# *Yesterday's Florida*

*Seemann's Historic States Series No. 1*

# Yesterday's
# FLORIDA

### by Nixon Smiley

E. A. Seemann Publishing, Inc.
*Miami, Florida*

Many individuals and institutions kindly supported the author's task in collecting photographs. The overwhelming majority of the photographs came from the State Photographic Archives at the Strozier Library, Florida State University, in Tallahasse, Mrs. Allen Morris, curator, acknowledged in the picture captions as (SPA). Other contributors were the following:

| | |
|---|---|
| (Burghard) | August Burghard, Fort Lauderdale, Florida |
| (Carson) | Don Carson, Miami, Florida |
| (DuBois) | Mrs. John DuBois, Jupiter, Florida |
| (Dunn) | Hampton Dunn, Tampa, Florida |
| (Eastern) | Eastern Airlines, Miami, Florida |
| (Edison) | Edison Winter Home, Fort Myers, Florida |
| (FCD) | Central and Southern Florida Flood Control District, West Palm Beach, Florida |
| (Fishbaugh) | W. A. Fishbaugh, Miami, Florida |
| (HASF) | Historical Association of Southern Florida, Miami, Florida |
| (Hoit) | The late Richard A. Hoit, Vero Beach, Florida |
| (JCC) | Jacksonville Chamber of Commerce, Jacksonville, Florida |
| (JHS) | Jacksonville Historical Society, Jacksonville, Florida |
| (Merrick) | Mrs. George E. Merrick, Coral Gables, Florida |
| (MBPD) | Miami Beach Publicity Department, Miami Beach, Florida |
| (MLS) | Mountain Lake Sanctuary, Lake Wales, Florida |
| (Marth) | Del Marth, St. Petersburg, Florida |
| (Miami Herald) | The Miami Herald, Miami, Florida |
| (Miami-Metro) | Miami Metropolitan Publicity Department, Miami, Florida |
| (Michel) | Mrs. Hedwig Michel, Estero, Florida |
| (Newton) | Jessie Porter Newton, Key West, Florida |
| (PBCHS) | Palm Beach County Historical Society, Palm Beach, Florida |
| (PCD) | Polk County Democrat, Bartow, Florida |
| (PRVHS) | Peace River Valley Historical Society, Wauchula, Florida |
| (Pan Am) | Pan American World Airways, Miami, Florida |
| (Perez) | Albert Perez, Miami, Florida |
| (Platt) | Frank Lester "Judge" Platt, Melbourne, Florida |
| (Romer) | The late G. W. Romer, Miami, Florida |
| (SAHS) | Saint Augustine Historical Society, St. Augustine, Florida |
| (SJPC) | St. Joe Paper Company, Port St. Joe, Florida |
| (Tebeau) | Dr. Charlton W. Tebeau, Coral Gables, Florida |
| (USCE) | U.S. Corps of Engineers, Jacksonville, Florida |
| (UWF) | University of West Florida, Pensacola, Florida |
| (Underwood) | T. C. Underwood, Wauchula, Florida |
| (W&L) | Stan Windhorn & Wright Langley, Key West, Florida |
| (Wright) | Hamilton Wright, Jr., Miami, Florida |

**Library of Congress Cataloging in Publication Data**

Smiley, Nixon, 1911-
   Yesterday's Florida.

   (Seemann's historic States series, no. 1)
   1. Florida--Description and travel--Views.
2. Florida--History--Pictorial works. I. Title.
F312.S63   917.59'03'0222   74-75296
ISBN 0-912458-38-0

Copyright © 1974 by Nixon Smiley
Library of Congress Catalog Card No. 74-75296
ISBN 0-912458-38-0

Manufactured in the United States of America

TO

*ALLEN MORRIS*

founder of the State Photographic Archives

# Contents

# *Foreword*

DOING *Yesterday's Florida*—selecting the photographs, preparing the captions, and writing a minuscule history of Florida as an introduction—has been one of the most challenging, fascinating, and satisfactory projects that I have ever undertaken. The idea of such a book of photographs, which essentially tells the story of Florida's past pictorially, grew out of the series of *Yesterday's* on the state's cities—Tampa, Miami, St. Petersburg, Clearwater, Sarasota, Key West—published by E. A. Seemann Publishing, Inc., since 1972.

The success of *Yesterday's Miami*, which I did in 1973, gave me the courage to think that such a book on the state, suggested by Seemann, would be possible. But the gathering together of illustrations of such diversity, covering so wide a geographical area over so long a period, would have been virtually impossible without the help of the State Photographic Archives. This superb collection is housed in the Robert Manning Strozier Library of Florida State University, Tallahassee.

A former newspaperman, Allen Morris, is the founder of the Archives. For a quarter-century Morris was recognized as a leading authority on "Cracker Politics," which also was the name of a column that appeared in many Florida newspapers. Since 1947 his *Florida Handbook*, revised every two years, has been the major unofficial source of information about Florida government and the activities of its many branches and departments. In 1966 Morris gave up his newspaper career for the prestigious job of clerk of the Florida House of Representatives.

In gathering material for the publication of his first *Florida Handbook*, Morris' major difficulty was finding illustrations. No central source covering the state existed. Morris began making his own collection, and, as a result of his state-wide contacts, the collection, which he housed in his office and at home, grew in size and acquired considerable value. Looking for a place to house the collection permanently and provide space for its continued growth, Morris approached the president of Florida State University, Dr. Doak S. Campbell. A deal was made in the early 1950s, and since that time the collection has grown to more than 65,000 photographs, many of them irreplaceable. Moreover, Morris and his wife Joan, librarian and curator, are still building the collection—a valuable gem for posterity.

If *Yesterday's Florida* is dedicated to Allen Morris, it is not only in recognition for his founding of the State Photographic Archives, but also because of a long-time friendship, dating back to 1935 when we worked together in the dusty, humid, and noisy wireroom of the Associated Press in the old Miami Herald building at Miami.

I regret that it is not possible to give credit to all the cameramen who took the photographs that made this book possible. Most of them, unfortuntely, are unknown, or there is uncertainty about whom to credit. The photographs have come from a great variety of sources—from families who inherited them, from newspaper files, from the National Archives, Library of Congress, historical societies, the military, and the anonymous files of commercial photographic firms employing several photographers, like Burgert Bros. of Tampa. It is embarrassing to be able to name so few: Charles Cottrell, Norm LaCoe, E. K. Hamilton, W. A. Fishbaugh, G. W. Romer, Ralph Munroe, Richard B. Hoit, A. S. Harper, Red Kerce, and Forest Granger.

Credit also is due to the following sources: Jacksonville Historical Society, *Florida Times-Union*, Peace River Valley Historical Society, *Florida Trend* magazine, Historical Association of Southern Florida, Palm Beach County Historical Society, *Tallahassee Democrat*, Miami-Metro Public Relations Department, Miami Beach Publicity Department, the *Miami Herald*, Edison Winter home; Mrs. John (Bessie) DuBois, Dena Snodgrass, Guy Wood, T. W. Underwood, Mrs. George E. Merrick, Hampton Dunn, Colonel Read Harding, Ralph Sumner, Del Marth, Jessie Porter Newton, University of West Florida, Judge James Knott, August Burghard, Don Carson, Mrs. Hedwig Michel, Stan Windhorn, and Wright Langley.

I want especially to thank Dr. Charlton Tebeau, chairman emeritus of the Department of History at the University of Miami, for his reading of the introduction before it went to the printer.


Nixon Smiley

Miami, 1974

# Yesterday's Florida

## From the Discovery to Spanish Cession

JUAN PONCE DE LEON, sailing northwest from Puerto Rico in search of fabulous Bimini, with its promises of riches and youth-restoring waters, came upon the mainland of North America on March 28, 1513.

"Believing this land was an island, they named it *La Florida*," wrote historian Antonio de Herrera, "because it had a very beautiful view of many cool woodlands . . . and because they discovered it in the time of the Feast of Flowers."

Upon turning south and passing Cape Canaveral, which Ponce named because of its numerous canebrakes, his caravels encountered a strong current flowing northward. Discovery of the Bahama Channel, or Gulf Stream, was to have a major influence on Spanish history in the New World, and particularly Florida. For this "ocean river" was to become the route of the Spanish treasure fleets, which, sailing from Havana, passed off the Florida coast, and, in the vicinity of Bermuda, set a course for the Azores and to Seville. To protect this route from preying French corsairs and English pirates, the Spanish were forced to establish St. Augustine.

To give Ponce de Leon credit for discovering Florida, however, is to ignore the existence of some 25,000 Indian inhabitants whose predecessors had arrived thousands of years before the Spanish. The early Floridians were hunters, pursuing such huge animals as the clumsy ground sloth and the mastodon. Their successors were farmers as well as hunters and fishermen. They left their ceremonial and burial mounds and enormous shell middens as evidence of their long residence. Unlike the docile Lucayans of the Bahamas, which the Spanish hauled off to work in the mines and the fields of Hispaniola, the Floridians were fiercely warlike. They slew several of Ponce's best soldiers

JUAN PONCE DE LEON *(left)* discovered Florida in 1513. Hernando de Soto *(right)*, who had helped Francisco Pizarro conquer Peru, landed at Tampa Bay in 1539 with the best-equipped army the Spanish were to send to the New World. Indian stories of golden wealth led De Soto on a wild-goose chase through the Southeast. He died on the banks of the Mississippi, disappointed and broken in spirit.

with their swift and accurate arrows, and mortally wounded Ponce himself during his second voyage in 1521.

"The time had not come," wrote historian Gonzalo Fernandez de Oviedo in commenting on Ponce's attempt to colonize Florida, "for the conversion of that land and province to our Holy Catholic Faith, since it was allowed that the devil should still possess those Indians with his deceits and the population of hell be swelled by their souls."

The devil was to remain on the side of the Indians, who upset the hopes of a succession of would-be colonizers and priests bent on subduing and converting them. Prior to the settlement of St. Augustine in 1565, every attempt made by the Spanish to gain a toe-hold in Florida had failed, and with enormous cost in men, ships, and equipment. Ponce de Leon, Panfilo de Narvaez, Hernando de Soto, and Tristan de Luna were typical of the restless, battle-hardened, and daring *conquistadores* who explored, conquered, and opened the New World for settlement. The defeat of the Moors at Granada in 1492 had released an energy matched by few other incidents in history. The captains of the Conquest and their successors overcame the enormous armies of the Aztecs and Incas to seize the gold treasuries of Mexico and Peru. They made Spain the richest nation in the world, and, for a time, the most powerful.

Why did the Spanish fail in their early efforts to colonize Florida? For one thing, the leaders frittered away their time and energy searching for gold and silver. Moreoever, the Indians were intractable, the soil unfamiliar, the climate, wilderness, and insects hostile. After De Luna's failure in 1561 to establish a colony at Pensacola, Philip II decided the country wasn't worth further efforts. But after learning that two shiploads of Huguenots under Jean Ribault had left France in 1562 to establish a colony in Florida, he changed his mind.

Ribault's colony failed, but in 1564 a second group of Huguenots under Rene de Laudonniere established a settlement on the south side of the St. Johns River, six miles from the mouth, and built Fort Caroline. This put the French in a perfect place to launch attacks on the Spanish treasure fleets. To meet this intolerable situation, Philip called upon one of his most trusted warriors, Captain-General Pedro Menendez de Aviles, ordering him to organize an expedition to drive the French out of Florida and to establish a permanent Spanish settlement. In exchange for the title of governor and the promise of rewards that went with it, Menendez agreed to bear the cost of the expedition.

Sailing from Santo Domingo on August 17, 1565, with five ships, 500 soldiers, 200 sailors, and 100 artisans, priests, women, and children, Menendez arrived off the coast of Florida on August 28, St. Augustine's day. On the same day seven French ships, with soldiers, settlers, and supplies to assist the small colony of Laudonnaire, arrived at the mouth of the St. Johns. In command was Jean Ribault, the French "corsair" most feared by the Spanish. Four of the ships, which drew too much water to cross the inlet bar, anchored outside.

Menendez, sailing northward, found a good anchorage on September 3, thirty-five miles south of the St. Johns. On the mainland was a Timucuan Indian village with a long communal house. Landing, Menendez made friends with Chief Seloy, who, hating the French because they had sided with his enemy, Chief Saturiba, gave the Spanish detailed information of Fort Caroline, some forty miles distant overland. Menendez, deciding he had found the perfect site for a settlement, named the place St. Augustine. But before beginning a settlement or fortifications, Menendez decided to tackle the first part of his mission—driving the French out of Florida. So he returned to his fleet and set sail. At the mouth of the St. Johns he found four French ships at anchor. Waiting until night, the Spanish moved in. Approaching, Menendez called out a threat to "hang and behead all the Lutherans I may find here either on land or on the sea," but the French cut their cables and hoisted sail. The Spanish gave up the chase at sunrise and returned to the St. Johns, but when Menendez discovered other French ships up the river, he sailed for St. Augustine. On the way the Spanish ships encountered squalls of

PEDRO MENENDEZ DE AVILES

LANDING at the St. Johns River in 1562, Jean Ribault remained only long enough to claim Florida for France, but he returned in 1565 to lose his life at the hands of the contesting Spanish. (SPA)

an approaching tropical storm. Landing at St. Augustine, Menendez moved into Chief Seloy's communal house and ordered work begun on a fort of logs and earth.

Ribault, meanwhile, returned to the St. Johns, where, at Fort Caroline, he organized an expedition to capture and hang the Spanish. On September 10 he sailed with over 600 men, leaving only a small garrison under Laudonnaire to protect the women and children and other noncombatants at Fort Caroline, among them Jacques le Moyne, the artist. By September 11, the storm had moved in, and St. Augustine was being lashed by hurricane winds.

Sensing that the situation was to his advantage, Menendez organized a battalion and at daylight struck·out across country in the wind and rain toward Fort Caroline, accompanied by Indian guides provided by Chief Seloy. Sur-

14

ON THEIR FIRST visit to Florida in 1562 the French made friends with the Timucua Indians who, for a time, provided them with grain and game after they returned in 1564 to build Fort Caroline on the St. Johns River.(LeMoyne)

prising the poorly guarded French fort, the Spaniards overcame the garrison and slew all the men who failed to escape. A number of women and children were slain before Menendez ordered a stop to the slaughter. Among those escaping were Laudonniere and Le Moyne, who, with other escapees, boarded two ships anchored in the river and sailed for France. Of the 240 Ribault had left in the fort, 132 had been slain. Menendez later permitted the surviving women and children to sail for France in a third ship with a French crew.

Concerned about the next move of the French fleet, now that the hurricane had passed, Menendez hurried back to St. Augustine. There he learned from Indians that the French ships had been wrecked on the beaches, and that the hungry survivors were gathering on the south side of an inlet below St. Augustine. Menendez hastened to the inlet with fifty men. There, after a conference, the French threw themselves upon Menendez' mercy and permitted themselves to be ferried across the inlet ten at a time—to be marched, hands tied, behind the nearby sand dunes where they were slain. Of 544 Frenchmen who survived the shipwrecks, 358 were slaughtered. Among them was Ribault, who, in addition to having his throat cut, had his head severed. The spot was to be forever afterward known as Matanzas—Place of Slaughter.

Although the French retaliated with a punitive expedition two years later, hanging sixty Spanish soldiers they captured at the former Fort Caroline, no attempt was made to destroy St. Augustine. But while the Spanish succeeded

15

CONSPIRING against one another and becoming involved with their Indian friends in war against the Indians' enemies, the French weakened themselves; within a year after their settlement in Florida they were ready to give up and return home. (LeMoyne)

PRESUMABLY alligators were eaten by the Timucuans as one is shown drying on this rack along with the carcass of a deer, rattlesnake, fish, and another unidentifiable animal. After being dried, the meat was hung in granaries with grain, beans, nuts, and other provisions. Despite the great Florida wilderness, food was never so plentiful that the natives could afford to relax long from the task of growing, hunting, or gathering roots and nuts. (LeMoyne)

ST. AUGUSTINE, drawn in 1671 from memory by an observer who erroneously recalled a string of hills, or low mountains, rising from behind the town. The rendition of the fort, which preceded Castillo de San Marcos, might be more accurate. Work on San Marcos was begun the following year. In 1668 Robert Davis, an English pirate, had sacked the town, killing a fourth of the 250 civilian residents.

in maintaining a colony at St. Augustine, Menendez' efforts to establish other settlements in Florida were costly and unsuccessful. Menendez sought to win over the several Indian tribes with the help of the Jesuits, but his efforts availed him nothing. Disheartened by Indian massacres, the Jesuits departed in 1572, to be replaced by Franciscan friars. Menendez died in 1574 at fifty-seven, impoverished by his Florida venture. Thereafter the king had to subsidize the Florida occupation with an annual grant.

The Franciscans built fifty missions in Florida and claimed 13,000 converts, although at a terrible price in dead friars. Integration of the natives into the Spanish economic life and social culture, as had been accomplished in Mexico, Central, and South America, never occurred in Florida. St. Augustine was able to do little for itself, except to build a powerful fort to protect the settlement from the assaults of pirates and the English colonists, as well as from the Indians. Succeeding governors were unable to steer Florida away from dependence on Spain, and in some years residents were on the verge of starvation by the time stores of wheat, flour, olive oil, and wine arrived from home. Even the missions were to a large extent dependent on these supplies, although converted Indians shared their food with the friars. Toward the end of the 1600s the Spanish were just beginning to discover the value of the prairies, canebrakes, and wiregrass for cattle raising. And in 1698 Pensacola was founded. But in 1702, Spain and England went to war and Florida was left to fend for itself against the onslaughts of the Carolina colonists.

Governor James Moore of South Carolina invaded Florida in 1702 and again in 1704. Although Fort San Marcos at St. Augustine held, Moore and his followers, including 1,000 Creek warriors, burned the Spanish missions and drove thousands of Catholic Indians northward to be sold as slaves. The surviving Franciscans and Spanish militia retreated to the protection of San Marcos and abandoned the rest of the peninsula. Only Pensacola, isolated because of distance, remained free from attack by the colonists. In succeeding years the Carolinian marauders ranged as far south as the Everglades in search of Indian slaves, cattle, and horses. And, if that wasn't enough to discourage Spanish efforts to hold Florida, England declared war on Spain again in 1739, in what was to be known as the War of Jenkins Ear. Governor James Oglethorpe of newly settled Georgia invaded Florida twice, devastated the countryside, and burned St. Augustine, but, like Moore, failed in efforts to take San Marcos. Spain finally lost Florida, in 1763, after the Seven Years War, exchanging the colony to England for Havana, which the British had captured in 1762.

Spanish power had been declining since 1588 when the Armada, sent by Philip II to destroy the growing British power under protestant Elizabeth I, met disaster. After that St. Augustine was merely an outpost, at the mercy of pirates who sacked the settlement several times before the building of Fort San Marcos in the late 1600s. Spain was too weak to challenge the establishment of English colonies in America. By 1763 most of the native Indian population had vanished, either as slaves or as a result of war and white man's diseases. When the 3,000 Spanish departed from St. Augustine they were accompanied by some eighty Catholic Indians and ninety-five free Blacks who were settled in Havana. A fewer number of Catholic Indians accompanied the 800 Spanish citizens departing from Pensacola. In all of Florida lived not more than 500 Indians when the British took over, a large percentage of whom were Seminoles, who had moved into the vacuum left by the vanished former Indians. The British divided Florida into two colonies, East Florida, with St. Augustine as the capital, and West Florida, with Pensacola the capital.

Florida began to show its first potential during the twenty years of British occupation. An offer of land grants attracted enterprising settlers from other colonies and developers from Britain. Plantations began to spring up along

JAMES OGLETHORPE

the St. Johns and other places where water transportation was available. But the greatest single effort was that of Dr. Andrew Turnbull who in 1768 sought to establish a 100,000-acre plantation at New Smyrna with 1,500 Mediterranean colonists. Although the project failed, the survivors, mainly Minorcans, remained to imprint their influence on the future of Florida. After the American Revolution the British returned Florida to Spain. With Spain on the south and west, and the independent American states on the north, England could see only trouble ahead if she should try to keep the territory. Florida simply wasn't worth fighting over. Moreoever, its maintenance had been costly. In 1783 the Spanish returned to St. Augustine, and most of the British colonists departed.

Spain's second occupation of Florida meant only trouble. Encouraged by the success of the British, the Spanish invited outsiders to colonize Florida. Many Americans, including those fleeing from the law, poured into Florida to occupy idle plantations left by the British. The American pioneers soon clashed with the Spanish and with the Seminoles, who by now occupied some of the better cattle lands in north Florida. In 1812, with encouragement by the United States, the Florida "Patriots" set up the East Florida Republic, chose trouble-maker John Houstoun McIntosh as president, and seized Fernandina. Spain, at war with Napoleon, was unable to meet the challenge. But when the Patriots went beyond the limited aims of President Madison and attacked St. Augustine, the United States disowned the "republic" and apologized to the Spanish governor. The United States was on the verge of war with Britain, and Madison was in no position to damage relations with Spain. But if the Spanish thought they had trouble with the East Florida colonists, that's because they hadn't met General Andrew Jackson.

During the War of 1812 the British took over the weak Spanish outposts of Mobile and Pensacola, and began arming Indians and Blacks to fight the Americans. Jackson set out for the coast at the head of an army of sharpshooting Tennessee volunteers, stopping on the way to rout the British-armed warriors of the Creek Nation in the Battle of Horseshoe Bend. Marching south to Mobile, Old Hickory beat off a British attack and occupied the city. Twenty-four hours later he took Pensacola. He then turned

A VETERAN of Napoleon's wars, Gregor MacGregor captured Fernandina in 1817 at the head of a rabble army. (SPA)

west again and marched to New Orleans ahead of the British, and dug in for an attack he knew was coming. After defeating the British in the Battle of New Orleans, Jackson returned home, but soon heard of more troubles in Florida.

An adventurer, Gregor MacGregor, with encouragement by American intriguers, invaded Spanish East Florida from Georgia in 1817 and took Fernandina without exchanging a shot. But the help he had expected failed to materialize, and, after an indecisive encounter with Spanish troops from St. Augustine, MacGregor departed, leaving Fernandina in the hands of fellow adventurers. Two days later the pirate Luis Aury landed with his cutthroats, took command, raised the Republic of Mexico flag, and encouraged resumption of illegal slave trade into the United States. This brought a U.S. Naval squadron, from which a garrison was landed to take command of Fernan-

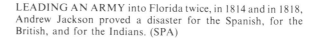

LEADING AN ARMY into Florida twice, in 1814 and in 1818, Andrew Jackson proved a disaster for the Spanish, for the British, and for the Indians. (SPA)

dina, but offering to turn it over to the Spanish whenever they could muster the forces to keep order. Meanwhile, encouraged by British intriguers, Seminoles went on the warpath into Alabama, terrorizing the countryside, and returning to their settlements in Florida with the scalps of their victims.

In 1818 Jackson was in Florida again, this time in pursuit of the Seminoles, as well as armed runaway slaves, alleged British spies, and lethargic Spanish officials who were unable or unwilling to maintain order in West Florida. Jackson burned the Seminole towns, hanged Indian leaders and two British subjects, then seized Pensacola and established his own authority.

Spanish protests availed nothing because Jackson was now an American hero whom not even President James Monroe would risk his political future in trying to discipline. Unwilling to go to war over Florida, Spain agreed in 1819 to cede the colony to the United States. In 1821 a change of flags was made at Pensacola and St. Augustine, and Jackson took possession as military governor of Florida.

## Indians, Statehood, and Civil War

WHEN THE UNITED STATES took possession of Florida in 1821, it was virtually as wild and undeveloped as it had been when Ponce de Leon landed, more than 300 years earlier. In all the 58,560 square miles of territory, extending 447 miles south from the St. Mary's River to Key West, and 361 miles west from the Atlantic to the Perdido River, lived only 12,000 inhabitants, half of which were Indians. The other 6,000 inhabitants were a diverse lot—plantation owners who had settled along the St. Johns during the British and Spanish occupations; farmers and cattlemen from Alabama, Georgia and the Carolinas; free blacks and slaves; survivors of the Minorcan colony at New Smyrna; runaway slaves, many of whom lived with or near the Indians; fugitives from justice; slave traders and slave hunters; swashbuckling adventurers; and pirates who preyed upon shipping along the Florida Keys and in the Gulf of Mexico.

What had happened to the estimated 25,000 Indians who once populated Florida, fishing the rich lagoons and river estuaries, hunting in the forests, or growing corn and pumpkins in forest clearings? Of those several tribes which claimed Florida in the early 1500s, only a few Calusa survived, living among the Everglades islands and in the Florida Keys. The Seminoles were themselves newcomers, mostly former Creeks and Miccosukees, who, having sided with the British and the Spanish in war and intrigue against the United States, could hardly expect sympathetic treatment by the new owners of Florida.

The Seminoles occupied the wild interior, while the white, slave, and free black populations were confined to the vicinity of Pensacola and northeast Florida. A few traders, adventurers, and fugitives lived at the mouths of rivers, such as the Apalachicola, Suwannee, and St. Marks, as well as in the regions of Tampa Bay, the Florida Keys, and Biscayne Bay. The interior began to draw settlers after Congress in 1824 appropriated $23,000 to build a highway from St. Augustine to Pensacola. Contractor John Bellamy followed the old Spanish Trail from St. Augustine to the former Spanish settlement of San Luis, the site of Tallahassee.

A number of towns soon sprang up along or near the St. Augustine Road—Tallahassee in 1824, Quincy in 1825, Monticello in 1828, Marianna in 1829, and Madison in 1831. Federal authorities in 1823 had forced a treaty on the Seminoles which required them to give up their lands in northwest and north Florida and move into an area of sand hills, flatwoods and swamp south of Gainesville covering nearly five million acres. This resulted in an influx of settlers which by 1830 had pushed Florida's population to 34,735—and still not counting the Indians.

War with the Seminoles was inevitable. Whites invaded the Indians' territory, hunting their game and driving off their cattle. The Indians retaliated with scalping raids against white homesteaders. A clamor went up from the settlers for Indian removal from Florida. The whites were anxious for an excuse to make war, while the Indians appeared to be determined to stand their ground and fight. To avoid further troubles, the Army established forts about the Seminoles' territory—to keep them confined as well as to keep

DEFIANT in the face of a choice between exile for his people or fighting, Osceola ignited a spirit of resistance in younger warriors that started the bloody Seminole War of 1835-42. (SPA)

FLORIDA'S second Capitol, built in 1826, occupied the site of the third, and present, Capitol in Tallahassee. This is how Comte de Castelnau saw it in 1838. It was razed in 1844 for the construction of a third Capitol. Florida's first Capitol was built of logs in 1824, on or near the present Capitol site. The town-site, laid out that year, was named Tallahassee, or "Old Fields," a Seminole name for the place. A post office was established in 1825. (SPA)

the whites out. Then, in 1832, Federal authorities met with the Indian chiefs at Payne's Landing on the Oklawaha River, and dictated a new treaty which essentially provided that the Indians would exchange their land in Florida for land west of the Mississippi.

Resistance to removal developed so strongly among the younger, warlike Seminoles, particularly Osceola, that older chiefs with cooler heads were brushed aside. And what was to be the most costly of the nation's Indian wars began on December 28, 1835, with the massacre of Major Francis L. Dade and all but one of the 108 officers and men under him. The war was to last seven years, to cost the lives of 1,500 service men and uncounted numbers of civilians and militia, to say nothing of Indians, and to drain the Federal treasury of $40 million. The United States was not to experience a similar war until it became involved in Vietnam, where the hit-and-run tactics of the enemy were similar to those used by the Seminoles.

Although the majority of the Seminoles were slain, died of exhaustion, or were shipped to what is now Oklahoma, 300 or more remained in the Florida wilds after the military walked away from the fight in 1842. But although the remaining Indians kept to the swamps, or to areas north of Lake Okeechobee unoccupied by whites, the pressure on them never ceased until another war was ignited in 1855. Chief Billy Bowlegs II and 123 of his followers were herded onto a boat and sent west, but the Civil War started before the remaining tattered Indians could be captured. These were to be forgotten for the next twenty years while the northern and southern states were engaged in fighting each other, or recovered from battle wounds and in reconstruction.

The Seminole War failed to hinder Florida's growth, and during the 1830s

23

the population increased from 34,735 to 54,477. One reason for this was an abundance of wagon roads the military built to virtually every part of the peninsula and the establishments of forts for the protection of settlers. After the war settlements grew up about the abandoned military sites and retained the names of the forts—like Fort Pierce, Fort White, Fort Myers, For Green, Fort Mead, and later Fort Lauderdale. But don't include Fort Lonesome, a crossroads settlement in Hillsborough County, named in the 1930s by Mrs. Dovie Stanaland "because the place was so lonesome."

Most of Florida's growth in the 1830s and 1840s took place in Florida's Panhandle, which had a cotton, lumber, and naval stores boom during those pre-Civil War years. The influential, dreaming of building an aristocratic planter society, sought to develop large plantations worked by slaves. Most of the planters grew cotton, in great demand at the time, but a few sugar plantations were developed in the peninsula, which was warmer than the Panhandle. Cotton ports like Apalachicola and St. Marks boomed. Cotton was shipped down the Apalachicola River from Alabama and Georgia, as well as from Florida, to be loaded on sea-going vessels. Florida's first railroad, with horse-drawn cars, was built from St. Marks to Tallahassee in 1834. St. Joseph, on St. Josephs Bay, was for a short time an important cotton port, but the community's short life, although historic, ended tragically.

St. Joseph was created as an "instant" city by former residents of Apalachicola after the United States Supreme Court gave the port to a land

LAST Florida Indian war, called the Third Seminole War, 1855-58, is said to have been started by Billy Bowlegs II after an Army survey party chopped up the Seminole chief's banana patch in the Big Cypress Swamp. Bowlegs retaliated by attacking the party, killing two men and wounding four. Sporadic fighting between whites and bands of Indians continued until 1858 when Bowlegs surrendered.

A MONUMENT is all that marks the site in once booming St. Joseph where Florida's first constitution was written between December 3, 1838, and January 4, 1839.

company. Earlier, during the second Spanish occupation, the trading firm of Panton, Leslie & Company had purchased from the Indians 1,250,000 acres of land extending from the Apalachicola River to St. Marks and reaching sixty miles inland. John Forbes & Company, which acquired this tract, in turn sold the land on which the growing town of Apalachicola was built to the Apalachicola Land Company. The residents refused to acknowledge the title, and the conflict wound up in court, which ended in 1835 with the land company as winner. Instead of paying the land company the exhorbitant prices asked for its lots, a major percentage of the residents, vowing they would "ruin Apalachicola," moved to near by St. Josephs Bay and started a new port. To attract cotton shippers, they built a railroad to Lake Wimico, a bayou of the Apalachicola River.

Although St. Joseph failed to ruin Apalachicola, it succeeded for a time in being Florida's most booming place—the "richest and wickedest city in the Southeast." It became Florida's first resort, sporting a horse track, gambling, and pleasure houses. The Mansion House, with its foreign decor, beautiful women and their cigar-smoking escorts, became notorious. With the deepest port between Pensacola and Key West, the largest vessels afloat could tie up to St. Joseph's 1,800-foot dock, and coastwise passenger ships operating between New Orleans and Charleston began stopping by, bringing new customers to the gambling and pleasure houses. In 1838 Florida held its first constitutional convention at St. Joseph, commemorated today by a monument and museum.

In 1841 an unusually virulent strain of yellow fever hit the community, striking down many of the town's leaders. Soon fewer than 500 persons remained. Nor did those who deserted return in the fall after the fever had subsided. Real estate prices collapsed, ships no longer stopped, and the town's bank failed, as did the railroad and other businesses. St. Joseph quickly became a ghost town. Many of the houses were dismantled and removed to Apalachicola. A hurricane and storm tide in 1844 destroyed what was left. But St. Joseph wasn't to be forgotten. The constitution adopted there became the basis for Florida's new government after it joined the Union on March 3, 1845.

25

DR. JOHN GORRIE (SPA)

Apalachicola, meanwhile, thrived as a cotton port until the beginning of the Civil War when the town was seized by Northern forces. Here Dr. John Gorrie, a physician, in 1845 discovered the process of making ice artificially from a machine he had built to cool the rooms of yellow fever patients. Gorrie, remembering from his high school physics textbook that air became heated while being compressed and cooled when released, built the first air-conditioner. He had not expected the machine to make ice, but it did that too. And it was then when Gorrie's troubles began. Like many another inventor, he spent his fortune and lost his health in pursuit of financial backing to manufacture ice commercially, and died in 1855 without receiving recognition for his discovery. Northern papers vilified him as being a hoax, and reminded readers that "only God can make ice."

Jacksonville, formerly Cowford, a cattle crossing on the St. Johns River, was established as a post office in 1824, but was to remain a sleepy town until after the Civil War when it became the resort capital of Florida. At the other end of the peninsula, Key West, like the Panhandle, had its great era during the three decades before the Civil War, when it boasted the highest per capita income in Florida.

Until 1821, when a squadron of Naval vessels was sent to Key West, the Florida Keys had been for years a favorite place for "wreckers" to prey on wrecked ships along the unmarked Florida Reef. The wreckers, mainly former New Englanders who had moved to the Bahamas during the Revolutionary War, were only a cut above pirates. During the second Spanish occupation the governor at St. Augustine had helped the American adventurer, Capt. John (Don Juan) McQueen, outfit a squadron to chase out the Bahamians and take over the salvaging of wrecks. But the colorful McQueen, onetime courier for George Washington, died of a heart attack on the eve of launching the campaign and the governor abandoned the project. The wreckers continued their operations, pouncing on wrecked or crippled vessels, salvaging the cargo, and taking it to Nassau or Havana. The presence of an American Naval squadron, first under Lieutenant Matthew C. Perry and them Commodore David Porter, with orders to put an end to piracy in the West Indies and the Gulf of Mexico, had a constraining effect upon the wreckers.

The Navy base was transferred to Pensacola in 1826, but the Federal government established a Superior Court in Key West in 1828, setting up rules under maritime law governing wreck salvage operations, and granting salvage licenses. Under the law, the salvage rights to a wrecked cargo went to the crew that got there first. Salvaged ships and their cargo were sold in Key West under the court's directions, and the proceeds distributed according to law. A colorful era developed as commerce between the Mississippi Valley and the East grew during that period before the building of the transcontinental railroads. Cargoes of laces, silks, wines, liquors, and silverware, as well as cotton, lumber, and naval stores, were shipped through the Florida Straits. In times of bad weather many ships piled up on the unmarked reefs. The wreck salvaging industry attracted many of the Northeast's top sailors, who made fortunes and built homes at Key West, with the familiar "captain's walk" crowning the roofs. Among the colorful wreckers was Captain Bradish (Hog) Johnson, a New Englander, who became "King of the Wreckers." But the one who made the most money was a supplier who disdained the sea—William Curry, who arrived in Key West from Green Turtle Cay in the Bahamas at fourteen. Curry, Florida's first millionaire, paid Tiffany $100,000 to make him a gold place setting, with gold serving bowls and a gold teapot. The erection of lighthouses in the Keys, together with the building of cross-country railroads and the development of the steamship, ended the "wrecking" era.

Although a full-fledged state in 1860, with fifteen years of self-government behind it, Florida was still little more than a wild frontier. Dueling was almost as much of a sport as a defense of honor. The slightest depreciating remark could get you an invitation to "fight it out" with dirks or pistols. The most famous duel was that between General Leigh Read and Colonel Augustus Alston, both political figures. So certain was Alston of victory that he arranged for a victory dinner at his home in Tallahassee. But it was Alston who died. Shortly thereafter a brother, Willis Alston, shot and killed General Read. Fleeing to Texas, Alston encountered a former resident of Tallahassee, a Dr. Stewart, with whom he argued. Both men drew guns and Alston got in the lucky shot. Arrested, the victor was taken to jail, where friends of Dr. Stewart broke in that night and riddled Alston's body with bullets.

With such a background of challenge and readiness for violence, it should be no surprise that Florida was the third Southern state to secede from the

CAPT. BRADISH (HOG) JOHNSON,
"king of the wreckers." (Newton)

Union—after South Carolina and Mississippi. While the election of Lincoln and the move of Northern abolitionists to free the slaves might have been the immediate cause of secession, the underlying cause was economic—the long growing tensions between the North and the South over trade, manufacturing, and tariffs. It was the political hot-heads, the ambitious business promoters, and opportunists who got Florida so quickly committed to a cause that made war unavoidable. The planters, as a group, were less than luke-warm to secession. So were some political leaders, including Senators David Yulee and Stephen R. Mallory. But they, like the planters, instead of trying to take leadership, allowed themselves to be led. Only three leaders who attended the secession convention in Tallahassee in January, 1861—former Governor R. K. Call, Buckingam Smith of St. Augustine, and Judge William Marvin of Key West—fought to keep Florida in the Union. Smith, a lawyer and historian, was not to be swayed from his position even after the war began. An early seizure of St. Augustine by Union forces kept him from being persecuted. Marvin was to serve as provisional governor of Florida for a short period after the war.

Florida, with its small population and lack of resources, was least able of the Southern states to fight a war. Moreover, its coastline was vulnerable, most of which was lost by the end of the first year of war. Northern forces oc-

THE CIVIL WAR in Florida was limited to fighting between small forces, like this engagement at the plank bridge over Big Creek in north Florida, on February 19, 1864. Only one major battle, Olustee, was fought in Florida. (SPA)

BLACKS SERVED in the Florida Legislature during the Reconstruction period imposed on the South following the Civil War. Although the Reconstructionists passed worthwhile legislation, including the establishment of a public school system, they were too progressive for the largely uneducated Floridians. Reconstruction ended in 1877 when the Democrats regained control of Florida and elected a Democratic governor. In the above group of legislators, photographed on the steps of the Capitol at Tallahassee in 1875, are three black members. (SPA)

cupied the important seaports and the peninsula was blockaded. The Union Navy, operating out of Key West, brought 229 captured blockade runners into port for disposal by Federal court. Still, blockade runners managed to escape capture and deliver cotton to Nassau, where it was sold to English buyers for enormous profit.

Florida's major contribution to the South's cause in the Civil War was its supply of food to the Confederate Army—beef and pork, cane syrup and sugar, as well as thousands of cowhides for shoes and saddles. Although the Union occupied Florida's major ports—or moved in and out at will—its attempts to gain a foothold inland were thwarted by hard-hitting raiders, like Captain J. J. Dickison. The only battle of any size fought in Florida, however, was at the Battle of Olustee on February 20, 1864, which the Confederates won. But leading Florida through the war had been so frustrating, wearing, and disappointing that as the end drew near Governor John Milton shot and killed himself.

Between 9,000 and 10,000 Floridians were serving in the Confederate Army at the war's end. How many were killed or died of disease is not known, but estimates place the number between 2,800 and 5,000. Those who returned found Florida greatly changed. The slaves had been freed. Farms were run-

UNION ACADEMY, for the education of children of newly freed slaves, was opened in 1866 at Gainesville by the Freedman's Bureau. Unpopular with local whites, the school depended entirely upon northern sources for support and for teachers. Beginning with elementary classes, the academy eventually offered high school courses, and added a normal school in the 1880s. Meanwhile, resistance among whites to the education of blacks gradually subsided, and in 1883 the Florida Legislature, at the urging of Governor Bloxham, provided funds for a normal school to train black teachers. The State Normal School for Negroes, forerunner of Florida A & M College, was opened in 1887, with fifteen students. (SPA)

down, herds depleted or non-existent. The names of old political leaders had been eclipsed and Union military authorities were in control. Thousands were destitute, particularly the newly freed blacks who not only were propertyless but almost 100 percent illiterate and without knowledge of the law or experience in a free society.

While the Freedmen's Bureau, established by Congress to help the former slaves, did much for Florida, the rise of radical Republicans in the political scene created disorganization and near chaos. Florida's die-hards, who couldn't believe the war was lost, contributed to the chaos by adopting a new constituion in 1865 which failed to give the black man the right to vote. This and similar arrogant, ill-conceived acts by the former Confederate states helped to galvanize support behind radical Republicans in the North, who in 1866 gained control of Congress. The result was a series of Reconstruction acts, aimed at humbling the losers as well as helping the newly freed slaves. Florida's constitution was invalidated and the blacks given the same voting rights as the whites. Moreover, whites who had voluntarily served in the

Confederate Army lost their voting rights. Florida's government fell into the hands of the "Carpetbaggers," radical Republicans from the North; "Scalawags," mostly poor, uneducated native whites, and former slaves. Of the forty-five delegates who attended a convention in 1868 for the writing of a new state constitution, were seventeen blacks, fifteen Carpetbaggers, and ten Scalawags.

The convention couldn't have been all bad, however, because the new constitution not only gave the black man voting rights, but established a public school system, and gave legal protection to labor. But the state was to remain in turmoil during Republican rule, with the rise of the Klu Klux Klan and widespread violence. Meanwhile, the section of the Florida Panhandle west of the Apalachicola River voted to secede from Florida and join Alabama. Republican Governor Harrison Reed appointed a commission to meet with a commission from Alabama in order to negotiate the annexation. A scandal developed after the Alabama commission was unable to account for the $10,-500 it had spent during the period of negotiations, however, resulting in the Alabama Assembly delaying action on the annexation proposal. It was not until 1883 that Alabama was ready to talk again about annexing West Florida, but by this time the annexationists had lost their ardor.

Although the Carpetbaggers were undoubtedly sincere in their liberal social and economic ideas, their thinking was too advanced for the time. Florida, with nearly half of its citizens illiterate and a large percentage of the remaining inhabitants poorly educated, was not ready for the ideals of the Northern progressives. The result was disillusionment by the blacks, who dropped out or were forced out of the political scene, and reaction by the Scalawags who joined the conservative Democrats to create a "Solid South"

GREATEST PUBLICIST of Florida after the Civil War was Harriet Beecher Stowe, whose *Uncle Tom's Cabin,* published in 1852, had caught the imagination of millions in America and Europe. This photograph, made about 1880, shows the Stowe family—Mrs. Stowe and her husband, the Reverend Calvin Stowe, center—sitting on the front porch of their winter home at Mandarin. From here the Stowes could look out across the placid St. Johns and watch the coming and going of steamboats. Mrs. Stowe's observations and experiences in Florida were published in America and abroad, bringing thousands to the St. Johns. The Stowe home was razed early in the 1900s, to be replaced by another house, but the great live oak still survives. (SPA)

against "Yankee Republicanism." Reconstruction ended in Florida with the inauguration in 1877 of Governor George F. Drew, first Democratic chief executive since the end of the Civil War.

Despite the empty Florida treasury and the state-wide bankruptcy at the end of the war, together with the turmoil resulting from a confused political era, Florida's population nearly doubled between 1860 and 1880—growing from 140,686 to 269,493. The Carpetbaggers who flocked to Florida at the end of the war soon were followed by capitalists who aided in the restoration of the railroads and in the building of a prosperous lumber industry. But what put Florida on the map was the discovery of its agreeable winter climate, the picturesque St. Johns River with its abundant wildlife, and the good hunting to be found in the countryside. Connected to the North by rail and by water, Jacksonville grew rapidly as Florida's tourist capital, and soon was the first city in Florida, a position it was to maintain as the "gateway" to the peninsula for many years to come.

## The Era of Tourism Begins

WHILE RAILROADS played a major role in the opening of the Florida frontier, the works of widely read authors did much to bring thousands of tourists into the state during the last quarter of the nineteenth century. Best known was Harriet Beecher Stowe, author of *Uncle Tom's Cabin,* who became a winter resident of Mandarin, on the St. Johns River, after the Civil War. Her book *Palmetto Leaves,* recounting her Florida experiences, was published in 1872. Sidney Lanier's *The Scenery, Climate and History of Florida,* which he wrote as a promotion for the Great Atlantic Coast Railway, was published in 1875.

These books presented Florida's climate, scenery, and wildlife in such a delightful way that readers were captivated. John and William Bartram, who visited Florida in the 1760s and 1770s, and John J. Audubon, who saw Florida in the 1830s, had pictured the wilderness as raw and unfriendly. While their writings may have made Florida attractive to other naturalists and adventurers, the average person was repulsed by the descriptions of teeming alligators in the rivers, stinging insects, and great forests inhabited by bears, panthers, wolves, snakes, and whatever other predatory varmints the imaginative reader could conjure in his mind.

Partly as a result of Mrs. Stowe and Lanier, whose works were widely read in Europe as well as in America, Florida, and particularly the St. Johns, flourished to become America's number one winter attraction. Palatial steamboats plied the St. Johns between Jacksonville and Orange Park, Man-

ENTERPRISE was a thriving community on the Saint Johns when the river was one of America's leading tourist attractions. After the era ended, Enterprise disappeared altogether—except for the cemetery and the layout of its streets. (SPA)

darin, Magnolia Springs, Green Cove Springs, Tocoi, Palatka, and Enterprise. The more adventurous boarded less ostentatious boats at Palatka for an exciting night trip up the winding, jungle-choked Oklawaha River to Silver Springs, or took a longer voyage up the St. Johns south of Lake George, to board a mule-drawn railway car for the eight-mile trip to Titusville, on the Indian River. Less adventurous was a side trip to St. Augustine, from Tocoi aboard a train of little more than Toonerville Trolley quality. Henry M. Flagler made this trip in 1883 while honeymooning with his second wife, and his infatuation with old St. Augustine was to have a major influence on Florida's history.

Many visitors decided to stay, Europeans as well as Americans, to plant citrus groves in Florida. Among them was Frederick Delius, sent from Bradford, England, by his capitalist father who figured that managing a grove in the Florida frontier would make the young man forget his interest in music. But Delius arrived at Jacksonville in the winter of 1884 to find the city more of a cultural center than his hometown. The city boasted a symphony orchestra, while the luxury resort hotels—Windsor, St. James, and Carlton House—had orchestras of their own, as well as French chefs and French waiters. His experiences in Florida, together with the sights of the St. Johns and the smells of the wilderness, had the opposite effect his father had hoped for, and when Delius returned to Europe he was on his way to becoming England's composer of the nineteenth century.

Florida was not so kind to everyone. Hamilton Disston, wealthy Philadelphia tool manufacturer, dropped a fortune in an effort to drain the rich glades of the upper Kissimmee Valley and about Lake Okeechobee. Disston in 1881 purchased four million acres of Florida swamp land for $1

33

THE WINDSOR, one of Jacksonville's leading tourist hotels, was built in 1875. (JHS)

GOVERNOR WILLIAM D. BLOXHAM

THE PLAZA, St. Augustine, in the 1880s. In the foreground is the city market, while in the background is the bell tower of the cathedral. (SPA)

34

million, most of which went to pay off the state's burdening debts. He succeeded in draining thousands of acres of wet glades in the Kissimmee-St. Cloud area—towns which he was responsible for creating—and began an extensive sugar operation. A depression in 1893 cut off his credit, however, and brought failure to the enterprise. Discouraged and remorseful, Disston shot himself.

Meanwhile, extension of railroads to the Tampa Bay area and down the East Coast to the Palm Beaches and Miami opened parts of the peninsula which heretofore had been isolated except by water. Florida's greatest railroad building era began in 1881 with the inauguration of Governor William D. Bloxham, who offered special bonuses in state-owned lands for every mile of new track laid. At the end of Bloxham's four-year term Florida had 1,348 miles of railroads, compared with 530 miles when he took office.

Big names in railroad building in the latter part of the 1800s were Henry B. Plant, Flagler, and Colonel William D. Chipley. Plant did his railroading in central Florida and on the Gulf Coast, Flagler on the East Coast, and Chipley in the Panhandle. Jacksonville was connected with Pensacola by rail in 1883, and with Tampa in 1884. Flagler, however, did not reach the Palm Beaches with his railroad until 1894, and Miami in 1896. The partner of John D. Rockefeller in the development of the Standard Oil Company built a string of resort hotels along the East Coast as he extended his railroad Southward, beginning with the Spanish Renaissance-style Ponce de Leon at St. Augustine, opened in 1888. He then bought and expanded the Ormond Hotel at Ormond Beach, opened the huge Royal Poinciana at Palm Beach in 1894, and the Royal Palm at Miami in 1897. Plant, meanwhile, opened the Moorish-style Tampa Bay Hotel in 1892 and the Belleview at Belleair in 1897.

Flagler and Plant never lived to see their enterprises pay off, but they, more than anybody else, were responsible for the opening of the East Coast and the Gulf Coast to development. Flagler's bridging of the St. Johns River in 1890 with a steel trestle made it possible for tourists to travel from northern cities to Flagler hotels without having to change trains.

Flagler planned to go no farther south than the Palm Beaches, but in the winter of 1894-95 two severe freezes wiped out Florida's citrus groves, together with a crop estimated at six million boxes. The economic effect not only was staggering, but had an immense influence on the state's development. It resulted in the shifting of the citrus industry from north to central Florida, and was responsible for the founding of Miami. The freeze did not reach Biscayne Bay, an area boasting only a few dozen families. So in late 1895 Flagler began extending his railroad southward from West Palm Beach, at the same time starting work on construction of the Royal Palm Hotel on land given him at the mouth of Miami River by Mrs. Julia Tuttle. When the railroad reached Miami in April, 1896, a thousand people were already in the newly laid out town to greet the first train.

FLAGLER BRIDGED the St. Johns River at Jacksonville in 1890, connecting his East Coast hotels with through Pullman service to northern cities. This bridge was a major step in the development of Florida's Gold Coast. (SPA)

It was like the end of an era and the beginning of a new one, but one more important event in Florida's nineteenth century was yet to happen—the Spanish American War. Although Key West served as a major Navy base during the war, Tampa became the disembarkation port for thousands of servicemen shipped to Cuba, including the Rough Riders who followed Colonel Theodore Roosevelt up San Juan Hill. Many of the men who camped in Tampa, or stayed at the Tampa Bay Hotel, would not forget, but, like the servicemen of succeeding wars, would return to call Florida home, thus helping to start off the new century with a sharp increase in the state's population.

## Florida in the Twentieth Century

THE OPENING of the lower coasts of Florida by railroads, together with the building of resort hotels, resulted in Jacksonville losing its position as the state's tourist capital. Then, in 1901, Jacksonville was virtually destroyed by a fire that swept through its downtown. A colorful era in the city's history was over. The resort hotels were in ashes, and, although the city was quickly rebuilt, it failed to recover its onetime glory.

The railroads rolled through Jacksonville, carrying train loads of tourists to Palm Beach and Miami, or to Tampa, Clearwater, St. Petersburg, Bradenton, and Sarasota. While a few winter residents returned each year to their homes along the St. Johns, the river had lost much of its appeal to sightseers. Most of the abundant wildlife that had made river trips so exciting had been decimated by sportsmen who used the once countless birds and alligators for target practice. Jacksonville would remain for nearly half a century as Florida's largest city, but in the meantime the populations of both lower coastlines were growing rapidly and eventually would pass that of northeast Florida.

Although the railroads already had opened the major geographical areas of Florida by the turn of the century, one project of importance remained—the building by Flagler of the Overseas Railway from the mainland to Key West. Begun in 1905, the most spectacular engineering project Florida was to experience before the Space Age, was completed in 1912. While the Overseas Railway was never profitable to the Flagler System, it proved to be Florida's greatest tourist attraction since the "discovery" of the St. Johns, and its influence on the growth of the state is incalculable. The fame of the project as the "eighth wonder of the world" spread throughout America and Europe. Most of the countless millions who read about it would never enjoy a ride on the "railroad that went to sea," yet it made Florida one of the interesting

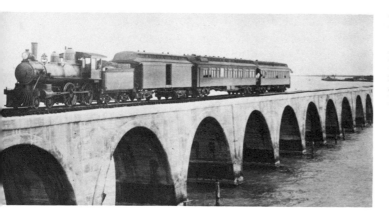

THE OVERSEAS RAILROAD to Key West, begun in 1905, was completed in 1912. Flagler's special train, with his private car in the rear, crosses the Long Key Viaduct on April 8, 1909, during an inspection trip. Flagler's private car is today on the grounds of the Henry Morrison Flagler Museum at Palm Beach. (SPA)

places in the world that most persons would like to go, if they had an opportunity.

During the first decade of the 1900s Florida's population increased 42.4 percent, from 528,542 to 752,619. Miami, with 5,471, was Florida's sixth city in 1910, behind Jacksonville, with 57,699; Tampa, 37,782; Pensacola, 22,982; Key West, 19,945, and St. Augustine, 5,494. During the next half century Florida was to experience a population gain of 450 percent, compared with a gain of 100 percent for the rest of the nation. But the lower East Coast counties were to gain 1250 percent during this period.

Another project which helped to sell Florida was the drainage of the Everglades, begun in 1905 during the administration of Governor Napoleon Bonaparte Broward. It wasn't just the digging of canals that turned millions of eyes toward Florida, but the sales of farmsteads in an agricultural "Eden" to countless numbers of people who had never seen the state. To pay for the expensive drainage project, the state sold large tracts of government-owned land to speculators, who subdivided it into small farmsteads and promoted them in Midwest newspapers. It ended in a major scandal, with the federal government sending to jail a scapegoat or two on charges of fraud. But Florida hadn't seen anything yet. The insanely wild speculation and promotion that marked the land boom of the 1920s would make the Everglades sales so unimportant that to historians they would go virtually unnoticed.

The Florida land boom began budding after World War I. Thousands of servicemen had been sent to Florida for training, specially in aviation. Many, like the servicemen who had seen Florida during the Spanish-American War, returned to live. While the boom spread through much of Florida, Miami was its capital. From a sprawling town of under 5,500 in 1910 Miami grew to a small city of just under 30,000 in 1920. But by the end of 1922 the population was estimated at 45,000, at 70,000 in 1923, and at 102,000 in 1924. But the greatest gain was recorded in 1925, when the population was estimated to have soared to 177,000. Five years later, after the "bust' and a destructive

38

hurricane, federal census counters could find only 142,739 permanent residents in all of Dade County, with 110,600 living in Miami. Jacksonville, with 129,459, still retained its lead as Florida's number-one city.

Florida had not recovered from the recession following the end of the boom when hit by the depression of the 1930s. Banks failed and railroads went bankrupt. Counties and communities defaulted in the payment of interest on bonds they had floated during the boom. Meanwhile, however, a New Deal Congress passed the Social Security Act, whose impact on Florida would be felt in the years ahead. And the decade passed, to be followed by World War II which was to change everything, including the way of life as well as the economy and society. Florida cities would become metropolitan, and people would stop bragging about which place was the largest. In fact, many cities were to become hard to find, having disappeared among urban sprawl that bled into other unidentifiable cities.

Although tourism was still Florida's mainstay after World War II, the state was becoming less dependent on this industry than in the past. For one thing, federal pensions were bringing many permanent residents, with their savings and Social Security checks. Moreover, the war had brought about new technology. Most of Florida's oranges were going into concentrated frozen juice, while the farms of south Florida produced the majority of the nation's winter vegetables during December, January, February, and March. With its phosphate reserves among the world's largest, Florida had become the

THE LAND BOOM of the 1920s brought tens of thousands of new people to Florida, and particularly to the Miami area. This is the intersection of East Flagler Street and First Avenue during the summer of 1925. Two years later you could have fired a cannon down Flagler Street in the summer without hitting anyone. (Miami-Metro)

nation's leading supplier of this vital mineral. And because of its abundant sunshine throughout much of the year, Florida became one of the top aviation states, with major post-war military bases established at Key West, Homestead, Orlando, Jacksonville, Tampa, Panama City, and Pensacola, while the Miami International Airport was becoming one of the world's leading air terminals. Cape Canaveral, selected for testing ballistic missiles, was to become the launching pad for America's Space Age.

Meanwhile the nation was beginning to enjoy a prosperity greater than anything the world had ever seen, and this was reflected in Florida by rapid growth and development much greater than that experienced during the boom of the 1920s. All was not well with the environment, however, but only a handful of conservationists were crying out against the wanton destruction of Florida's natural resources and the degradation of the air and water by pollutants. The time was to come when the public would awaken and its demand for controls would explode into the Environmental Revolution of the 1960s. But before the quiet revolution could run its course, the nation was to face still another major problem—shortages of fuel to operate motor vehicles and scarcity of petroleum-derived materials for industry. By 1974 the nation was facing problems almost as great as those accompanying World War II, with the prospects of immense changes in a way of life, both at the economic and social levels. And no matter how the solutions were made, Florida would be affected.

# Florida from 1821 to 1875

SPAIN LEFT few relics behind when Florida was ceded to the United States in 1821. St. Augustine, Fernandina, and Pensacola were the principal communities. But only St. Augustine was to retain much of its original charm—like Charlotte Street, with its Spanish balconies and with entrances that opened into the street.

CASTILLO DE SAN MARCOS at St. Augustine was the most important historic relic left behind by the Spanish. Built between 1672 and 1700, the fort had the unique history of having never been taken by an enemy. The thick walls, built of coquina, a stone comprised of small seashells fused together by dissolved calcium were impregnable to the cannon in use before 1860. This photograph was made in 1901. (SPA)

ENTRANCE to the moat at San Marcos in the 1890s. These coquina columns are much the same as they were when constructed some 200 years earlier. The fort is today a National Monument. (SPA)

OLDEST HOUSE now standing in Pensacola is the brick-stuccoed Barkley House, at 410 S. Florida Blanca Street. Built during the second Spanish occupation, 1783-1821, the owner was George W. Barkley, an English trader. (SPA)

PENSACOLA'S early houses, mainly of wood, fell prey to time and to men's inclination to knock down and rebuild. This brick house which was headquarters for Panton, Leslie & Company, an Indian trading firm organized during the British occupation of Florida, 1763-1783 was dismantled in the early 1900s. (SPA)

WAR BETWEEN the Seminoles and the whites was inevitable after Florida became a United States possession, and settlers from Georgia and the Carolinas poured into the new territory to challenge the Indians for land. This attack by Seminoles on a block house was drawn by an artist in 1837 and published in Charleston, S.C. (SPA)

THE NATIONAL IMAGE of the Seminole was that of a savage without soul, bent on looting, murder, and scalping. Nor was the national conscience bothered by the seizure of the Indians' land by white settlers and efforts by the government to tear the Indians from the territory they knew and ship them to a strange land west of the Mississippi. Even as late as the 1880s, the Seminoles were pictured as cruel and inhuman, as illustrated in this scene of a massacre and scalping during the Seminole War. The engraving appeared in a book, *The Romance and Tragedy of Pioneer Life,* by Augustus L. Mason, published in 1883. (SPA)

THE SEVEN YEARS' Seminole war was ignited on December 28, 1835, after a battalion of troops, en route from Fort Brooke at Tampa *(below)* to Fort King in Ocala, was massacred by a band of Seminoles near the present site of Bushnell. (SPA)

THE MAJOR BATTLE of the Seminole War occurred near the northeast shore of Lake Okeechobee on Christmas Day, 1837, when an army of 1,000 under Colonel Zachary Taylor encountered 400 Indians who stood and fought. Although twenty-six whites were slain compared with eleven Seminoles, the Indians gave ground and withdrew. While the battle was far from decisive, Taylor emerged the only national hero of the war. The war continued, however, for another five years. (SPA)

APALACHICOLA in 1837, when this drawing was made by H. A. Norris, was among the larger cotton ports on the Gulf of Mexico, even outranking its rival St. Joseph. Some 50,000 bales of cotton a year were shipped down the Apalachicola River to the port town of Apalachicola, from where it was shipped by ocean-going vessels to Eastern cities and to Europe. (SPA)

KEY WEST had but a few hundred inhabitants in 1838 when sketched by Francis Conte de Castelnau, but the salvaging of wrecks along the Florida Reef was making it the richest place per capita in the state. (SPA)

"WRECK ON THE REEF" was a familiar cry among the wreckers in the Florida Keys during the 1830s and 1840s, as increasing numbers of ships passed through the Florida Straits before the markings of reefs and shoals with lighthouses. And even after the erection of lights many ships were driven onto the jagged coral by storms. The four-masted schooner of a later vintage, (left) which foundered on Tennessee Reef early in the 1900s, is one of hundreds of such ill-fated ships. These ships, like the one below, were swarmed over by licensed wreckers who, after removing cargo and stripping the vessels, left them to the mercy of the waves, sea-worms, and rot. (SPA)

LIGHTHOUSES have played a greater role in Florida's past than historians have given credit. Soon after Florida was acquired in 1821 the United States began building lighthouses to mark dangerous reefs and shoals. Lighthouses were increased along the peninsula's 1,350 miles of coastline as shipping gained between the Atlantic and the growing Gulf and Mississippi Valley areas. Cape Florida, above, was built in 1825. Seminole Indians burned out the interior in 1837. The keeper managed to save his life by lying on a platform outside the tower and just below the light, but his helper was slain. The light was extinguished in 1878 upon completion of more sophisticated lights on the Florida Reef. (SPA)

STYLES among Florida lighthouses varied immensely. Left is the multiple steel tower at Sand Key, at right the tower at Anclote. (SPA)

KEY WEST lighthouse *(below, center)* was built after a hurricane in 1846 destroyed an earlier one, killing the keeper and six members of his family. No longer active, it is today part of the Lighthouse Military Museum, of which the adjacent building, formerly the lighthouse keeper's home, is a part. (SPA).

JUPITER lighthouse *(below, left)* was built before the Civil War. Extinguished by Confederate forces, it was re-lighted after the war. When keeper James Armour brought his bride, the former Almeda Carlile, to Jupiter in 1867 she was the only white woman living within a radius of 100 miles. Jupiter light is still active. (SPA)

REBECCA SHOAL lighthouse *(below, right)* in 1885 when this photograph was made, was a curious two and one-half story house set upon steel piling, with the light rising from a captain's walk at the spex of the hip roof. (SPA)

CATERING to members of the Legislature and others in Tallahassee on government business, the Morgan Hotel was built in 1834 and expanded. Located at the southwest corner of Adams and Pensacola streets, it began life as Brown's Inn, then became the City Hotel and the Adelphi before Morgan was tagged onto it. The wood structure was destroyed by fire in 1886. (SPA)

AGITATION for statehood after the adoption of the first Florida constitution at St. Joseph in 1839 resulted in Congress appropriating $20,000 for the building of a new Capitol at Tallahassee. The old Capitol, built in 1826, was razed and a new one started, but funds ran out in 1841 and the territorial government had to ask Washington for another $20,000. The Capitol was completed just prior to Florida's being admitted to the union as the twenty-seventh state on March 3, 1845. The building was to remain like this until 1891 when a cupola was added. (SPA)

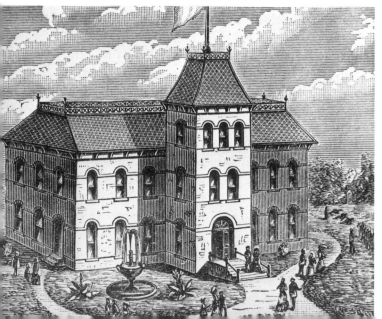

EAST FLORIDA SEMINARY, erected in 1853 at Gainesville, marked the beginning of state support for higher education. It was a forerunner of the University of Florida, established in 1905. The West Florida Seminary, opened at Tallahassee in 1857, became the Florida State College for Women in 1909. Upon becoming co-educational in 1947 the name was changed to Florida State University. (SPA)

PRINCESS MURAT, widow of Prince Achille Murat, a nephew of Napoleon Bonaparte, purchased this cottage, Bellevue, in 1854 after the death of her husband. The prince, who settled near the state capital in 1825, had gone so deeply in debt in the operation of his 4,040-acre estate, Econchatti, with its more than 100 slaves, that his widow was forced for a time to give up her mansion and live at modest Bellevue. The Murat mansion is gone, but Bellevue survives. In 1967, after the house faced destruction as a result of expanding Tallahassee, it was moved to a site on the grounds of the Tallahasee Junior Museum and restored. The Princess Murat house is believed to have been built in the 1830s. (SPA)

GRAND STYLE atmosphere sought by antebellum planters lingers in the ruins of the Gamble Mansion at Ellington, near Palmetto, when this photograph was made in 1902. Built between 1845 and 1850 by Robert Gamble, it was the center from which a 3,500-acre plantation was administered, including 1,500 acres of sugarcane worked by slaves. In 1925 the Judah P. Benjamin Chapter of United Daughters of the Confederacy purchased the mansion for $3,200, minus the original acreage, and gave it to the State of Florida, which restored and maintains it. (SPA)

49

STATELY COLUMNS in the wilderness (right) are all that remain today of Verdura, largest and most magnificent antebellum home built in Florida. Verdura, with fifteen rooms and a dozen fireplaces, was built twelve miles southeast of Tallahassee in the early 1830s by Major Benjamin Chaires. Chaires is believed to have died of yellow fever in 1838. The 10,000-acre plantation went to seed after the Civil War and the neglected mansion burned in 1885. (SPA)

LANDING of reinforcements at Fort Pickens, on Santa Rosa Island, at the entrance to Pensacola Bay, four days after the beginning of the Civil War, destroyed Florida's chance to seize the important Federal fortification. Florida had begun seizing Federal military installations immediately after voting to secede in January, 1861, taking over Fort Clinch at Fernandina and Fort San Marcos at St. Augustine, as well as the Federal arsenal at Chattahoochee with a handsome supply of munitions. Federal troops, occupying Fort Pickens, Fort Taylor at Key West, and Fort Jefferson in the Tortugas, at the beginning of the war, held them throughout the conflict. Note in the upper drawing a horse is being lowered into the water with the aid of a sling, to swim ashore behind the boats, as shown in the lower scene. The troops, with their horses and equipment, marched along the beach to Fort Pickens. This landing took place on April 16, 1861. Fort Sumter, in Charleston Bay, had been bombarded by the Confederates on April 12, igniting the Civil War. (SPA)

50

ALTHOUGH BEGUN in 1845, Key West's Fort Taylor was not completed until after the beginning of the Civil War. The fort was occupied by Federal troops in 1861 and work was begun on the construction of two Martello towers for the further protection of Key West, an important base for operations against blockade runners. By the time Fort Taylor was completed, it was obsolete. Modernized during the Spanish-American War, some 200 Civil-War-vintage cannon were buried with 200,000 cannonballs, rubble, and sand in the first-floor casements, new battlements constructed, and twelve-inch guns mounted. Spoil from dredging about the Key West Naval Station eventually filled the 1,000-foot lagoon between the fort and the mainland, and Fort Taylor, once an island stronghold, became a pile of commonplace masonry. But in the 1970s efforts were being made to recover the buried cannon, the largest collection of old cannon in the world, and restore the fort to some of its former grandeur. (SPA)

A MAJOR ENGAGEMENT in Florida during the Civil War was the Battle of Olustee, fought near Lake City on February 20, 1864. Federal forces numbered 5,500, one-third of which were black troops, while Confederate forces number 5,200, two-thirds of which were Georgians rushed to assist the Floridians. The Federal objective was to cut off supplies—cattle, hides, cotton, salt and some grain—from Florida to Confederate forces in other states. Like other Union attempts to gain a foothold in interior Florida, the effort failed. Union losses with 203 killed, 1,152 wounded, and 506 missing, while Confederate losses were 93 killed, 847 wounded, and six missing. (SPA)

ENTRANCE to Pensacola harbor was sharply contested by Union and Confederate forces at the beginning of the Civil War, and the first engagement of the war in Florida was fought here on the night of September 2, 1861. No blood was shed, but two weeks later three Union soldiers were slain and eight wounded during an attack on the Confederate ship *Judah*, fitted out as a blockade runner. The ship was set afire. Then, on October 9, a Confederate force of a thousand engaged Billy Wilson's Zouaves, an elite Union unit, in a battle on Santa Rosa Island four miles east of Fort Pickens. The Union claimed victory while the Confederates claimed they destroyed large stores of Federal provisions, equipment, and ammunition. Confederate losses were eighteen killed, thirty-nine wounded; Union losses fourteen killed, twenty-nine wounded, and twenty captured, including a major. In the illustration (*above*) which appeared in the *New York Illustrated News*, a major battle appears to be in progress rather than a skirmish. *Below*, a Confederate garrison pretends to guard the entrance to Pensacola Bay from Warrington. But Confederate forces were needed elsewhere, and by 1862 most of the 5,000 troops which had been used in the defense of Pensacola had been transferred to more active fronts, particularly Virginia. Upon occupying Pensacola, Federal troops found the place practically deserted, even by civilians, and everything of any military value removed. (SPA)

A DWELLING of the Spanish era (*above*) served as headquarters for the post quartermaster of Federal forces occupying St. Augustine during the Civil War. Dated December 11, 1864, the photograph shows the architectural style in the old city. *Below*, Union artillerymen stand by guns set up in the courtyard of Fort San Marcos. Note the tents on the rampart. (SPA)

UNION FORCES held key Florida ports throughout the Civil War, or moved in and out at will. Jacksonville (*above*) was occupied four times. The stars and stripes fly over the National Hotel during one occupation. The signal tower (left) erected in Jacksonville's public square, now Hemming Park, was one of a series of such towers which gave the Union forces instant communication with a blockading fleet. The lookouts were frequent targets of Confederate snipers. *Below*, Union troops marching in Fernandina during war. (SPA)

WINTRY SCENE at Jacksonville in 1865, with a family strolling in front of St. Paul's Methodist Church and leafless chinaberry trees, has all the grim character you would expect as the end of the long and bloody Civil War approaches. The South is busted. Everyone is broke. Slaves and their former masters are almost in the same situation—except that one hundred percent of the blacks are illiterate, while two-thirds of Florida's whites can at least read and write. After leading Florida through four years of frustrating war, Governor John Milton (*right*) shot and killed himself—on April 1, 1865, the day before Lee surrendered to Grant in Virginia.

55

VIEW OF TALLAHASSEE, sketched just after the Civil War, shows a Federal troop cantonment in the city, upper left, near the American flag standard. A Union flag also flies over the Capitol, where a Confederate flag had flown throughout the war. This scene, which appeared in Frank Leslie's *Illustrated Newspaper* in 1868, at first glance seems to depict the Capitol from the northeast. Instead, you are looking from the southwest. The Capitol then had matching colonnaded fronts on the east and west. The west colonnades, depicted here, were to be removed in 1921 during one of several expansions of the Capitol building. The slender steeple is that of the First Presbyterian Church. Tallahassee was the only Confederate state capital east of the Mississippi which did not fall into Union hands during the war. (SPA)

FORT JEFFERSON (*above*), built at Dry Tortugas, sixty miles west of Key West, between 1846 and 1865, was the United States' most costly bastion of the nineteenth century. Covering sixteen acres, forty million bricks were used at a cost of a dollar each for transportation alone. Its 243 large-caliber guns were never fired, and by the end of the Civil War the fort was obsolete—except as a prison. Dr. Samuel A. Mudd (*left*), who set the broken leg of John Wilkes Booth, assassin of President Lincoln, was imprisoned here. He was pardoned in 1869 by President Grant. Fort Jefferson is today a national monument, which includes all the islands of the Dry Tortugas group. It is reachable by boat or seaplane. (SPA)

FLORIDA "CRACKERS" were looked upon by visitors from out-of-state as a sub-human species. George M. Barbour, author, described them in the 1880s as "clay eating, gaunt, pale, tallowy . . . stupid, stolid . . . poor white savages." To the blacks they were known generally as "poor white trash." The Cracker, as depicted by Barbour, would survive until the 1930s when the federal-supported lunch program was started in public schools, to provide children from poverty-ridden families with at least one adequate meal a day. The poor whites proved not to be a distinct species after all, but undernourished people trying to live off land that failed to provide sufficient minerals and vitamins in the food produced. With better nutrition the "breed" disappeared. And after World War II all native Floridians were to become known as Crackers, to separate them from the more numerous newcomers. (From *Florida for Tourists, Invalids, and Settlers*)

CRACKER FAMILIES, many of them illiterate like the blacks, had little to boast of after the Civil War, except a stubborn independence. The log house with mud chimney (*left*) was a common Cracker-house style. At right is a board-and-batten house, the home of a black family. The framing and the boards were usually of rough-sawed pine, and the houses, without paint, decayed within a few years in Florida's warm and humid climate. (SPA)

POETIC LICENSE was taken by photographers after the Civil War to picture the carefree life of the black man among the picturesque surroundings of the Florida wilderness—like the derby-topped old gentleman fishing in the St. Johns River. But life was grubby for most former slaves after the war. Illiterate and ignorant of the ways of a free society, most of the older blacks lived out their days in whatever shelter they could find—like the old cabin photographed near Tallahassee—usually on some white family's farm. A few chickens, a garden patch, and whatever fish they could catch in lakes and streams, provided them with the barest kind of a living. (SPA)

FISHING ON THE ST. JOHNS.

A BIG DAY it was in Tallahassee in 1874 when Harriet Beecher Stowe, author of *Uncle Tom's Cabin* and an ardent promoter of Florida, visited the state Capitol. Marcellus L. Stearns, last of the carpetbagger governors, stands in the central part of the steps, awaiting the opportunity to shake hands with the famous woman. Most of the onlookers are watching the camera instead of Mrs. Stowe. Note the unkempt condition of the grounds. Looks like some carpetbagger or scalawag would have raked the leaves and trash from the walk in front of the steps. (SPA)

COW FORD was the name of a crossing on the St. Johns River at the present site of Jacksonville when Florida became a United States possession in 1821. Here was the narrowest location in the river for a hundred miles, where the stream was shallow except for a deep, swift channel in the middle. Cows and horses were waded to the channel, then forced to swim to shallow water on the other side. A Kings Road was built from St. Augustine to Georgia by way of Cow Ford during the British occupation, 1763-1783. Jacksonville, in honor of General Andrew Jackson, was founded in 1822, and that year local citizens petitioned John Quincy Adams, secretary of state, to establish a port of entry here. A Jacksonville post office was established in 1824, a year before one was established in Tallahassee. But Jacksonville made little growth until after the Civil War, when the city became the capital of a thriving tourist industry on the picturesque St. Johns. (JHS)

# Tourism and Development, 1875 to 1900

JACKSONVILLE'S WATERFRONT on the St. Johns in 1886. (SPA)

DISCOVERY of the St. Johns River after the Civil War as a tourist's paradise was to set the pace for a development that would make Florida the leading resort state in America. Above is busy, growing Jacksonville in 1876, eleven years after the end of the war—now a bustling port and rail junction, together with luxury hotels. Below is Jacksonville's first Union Station. (SPA—JHS)

60

CONTINENTAL cuisine was the fare at Jacksonville's hotels during the great tourist boom in the 1870s and 1880s. Most hotels had their own orchestras. Above is the National Hotel, below the St. James. (SPA)

WHO COULD DOUBT the popularity of excursions on the St. Johns in the 1880s after seeing this photograph of the steamboat *Sylvester (above)* during a trip up river? The *Frederick DeBary (left)* plied the river between Enterprise and Jacksonville. Below, the *Florence,* docked at Green Cove Springs, stopped at Palatka, Mandarin, Toci, and Orange Park. (SPA)

INVALIDS—rheumatics, the crippled, aged and infirm—came to Florida in wintertime to bathe in the 78-degree mineral water of Green Cove Springs *(below).* And they claimed they felt better after taking the "cure," which included drenching their gullets with the sulfurous-smelling water. In the evening they ate sumptuous meals at the Union Hotel *(above)* and the Clarendon, after which the wagering types retired to the gambling casinos. Horse racing was held once a week in Sarasota Street, when townspeople and visitors got together and "lived it up." (SPA—JHS)

THE GREATEST ADVENTURE of any Florida vacation in the 1870s and 1880s was to take a steamboat trip up the winding Oklawaha from the St. Johns to Silver Springs. Among those making the trip was Sidney Lanier, who, inspired, sought to inspire others, and succeeded. Above a venturesome crowd has boarded the *Okeehumkee* at Palatka for an overnight trip to Silver Springs. Below, the *Metamora* churns the water as it makes one of the countless bends the river takes through the Oklawaha wilderness. (SPA)

NATIVES along the Oklawaha made a living cutting fat pine wood for the steamboats which made stops to replenish supplies of fuel. This firewood station might have been at Orange Springs, a ferry crossing. Below, the Morgan House at Silver Springs, where steamboats reached at breakfast time after a night's trip up the Oklawaha River and Silver Run. The hotel burned in the 1890s. (SPA)

65

SPORTSMEN as well as sightseers discovered Florida, which bode ill for the future of the northern part of the state as a tourist attraction. On river excursions sportsmen lined the decks of steamboats and fired at every living thing that showed itself—ducks, wading birds, alligators. The dead and crippled creatures were left where shot. Despite the shrill cries of protest by Harriet Beecher Stowe, Florida's first conservationist, the shooting continued until the wildlife virtually disappeared from the St. Johns and Oklawaha, after which interest in the rivers by tourists waned. Inland areas also offered an abundance of shooting and hunting. Above, a quail shooting party prepares to leave Moore's Hotel in Hawthorne. With no limit on game, sportsmen shot as long as the ammunition lasted. Below, these sportsmen are proud of the 684 doves shot in a single day at the Anthony Stock Farm near Ocala. (SPA)

LA SPORTSMEN, 684 DOVES IN ONE DAY'S HUNT ON THE

CURLICUED architecture had its day along the busy St. Johns as hotels sought to outdo each other in decorative extravagance. DeBary Hall (above), a home built on the St. Johns near Enterprise in 1871 by Count Frederick DeBary, a wine merchant, is conservative compared with the Nichols House (right) built at Jacksonville in the 1880s. But even more ornamental is the Magnolia Hotel (below), built at Magnolia Springs at the turn of the century. Only DeBary Hall still stands, a state-maintained historic landmark at the town of DeBary. Both Magnolia Springs and its hotel have vanished, as has old Enterprise.

RAILROADS and railway services were greatly expanded throughout much of the state in the 1880s and 1890s. Moreover, the rail lines opened new territories, including the lower East Coast and the lower Gulf Coast. Prototype of the 1880s trains was this cabbage-stack engine and passenger car of the Florida Railway & Navigation Company, photographed in Tallahassee at the foot of Capitol Hill in 1886. The gentlemen lined up for the photograph are inspectors—probably investment bankers, executives, board of directors members, and important stockholders. (SPA)

A SHORT LINE of seven and one-half miles, the Jupiter & Lake Worth Railroad proved nevertheless to be a big money maker. Known as the Celestial Railroad, because it went from Jupiter to Juno by way of Venus and Mars, the line and rolling stock cost $70,000 in 1889. Charges were 20 cents a hundredweight for freight and 75 cents for passengers. Then, after Henry Flagler decided in 1893 to extend his railroad to the Palm Beaches and build the Royal Poinciana Hotel, the Celestial Railroad collected $96,000 in a few months for hauling building supplies. Although Flagler's route put the line out of business after it reached West Palm Beach in 1894, the Celestial Railroad's owners already had made a killing. (DuBois)

THE RAIL TRIP from Tocoi on the St. Johns to St. Augustine was but fifteen miles, but when these cars were mule-drawn time could have been saved by walking. (Note the single tree below the figure "1" on the first coach, to which the mule was hitched.) William Astor bought the line in 1876, laid steel rails, and replaced the mule power with steam locomotives. Flagler, on a honeymoon to the St. Johns in 1883, traveled by Astor's train to St. Augustine. Falling in love with the old city, he began investing in Florida the millions he had made in the Standard Oil Company. (SPA)

AS TRAIN TIME approaches in Orlando, in the 1880s, hacks, buggies, wagons, and a mule-drawn streetcar gather at the station to pick up passengers, freight, and the mail. (SPA)

INTERIOR FLORIDA began to thrive as newcomers—many of them former tourists—moved in to clear rich hammocks and plant citrus. Among the growing towns was Ocala, near Silver Springs, where, above, a parade celebrates some now unknown occasion. In the background is the many-colonnaded Ocala House. Below, Moore's Hotel at Hawthorne was a favorite place for sportsmen and for persons looking for an opportunity to settle in Florida. Many of the settlers, who planted oranges, would see their groves wiped out by the 1894-95 freezes. The climate of north Florida proved to be too cold for citrus. But in this photograph, made in the 1880s, the bewhiskered gentleman, right, stands behind a citrus tree. (SPA)

ROADS were unpaved and few bridges existed in the 1880s—and bridges that did exist, like this one at Hawthorne, were usually privately built. This bridge is to get customers to Morrison's water mill, beyond the stream, where the post office also is. Founded as Jamestown in 1879, the name was changed to Hawthorn in 1880, after James H. Hawthorne, the founder, but was misspelled. The spelling was corrected in 1950 when the Post Office Department in Washington was persuaded to add an "e." (SPA)

FOUNDERS of Moore's Hotel at Hawthorne in 1883, William Shepard Moore and Virginia McGraw Moore, right, dressed for the photographer in the styles of that era. Below, the Moores take their five children out for a buggy ride behind the old gray mare.

SPANISH architecture may have survived in St. Augustine because of the poverty of the inhabitants after Florida became a United States possession and the capital was moved to Tallahassee. There just wasn't any money to tear down and rebuild. Charlotte Street (above) was typical of the Oldest City immediately after the Civil War, when boat building and fishing were about the only industries. Its discovery by tourists in the 1870s was to help the city to prosper, and at the same time to emphasize the value of Spanish heritage. At right is a portion of the city with its huddled little houses in 1887, while below is the Cathedral during the Civil War when St. Augustine was occupied by Union forces. (SAHS)

MINORCANS, survivors of an ill-fated colony at New Smyrna in the late 1700s, dominated the political life of St. Augustine for half a century after it became a United States possession. Pedro Benet *(left)*, known as "King of the Minorcans," was the grandfather of Stephen Vincent Benet, author of the famous poem, *John Brown's Body,* while Charles "Bossy" Benet *(below),* St. Augustine's colorful marshal, ordered city councilmen to keep quiet while he was talking.

THE OLD GATE at St. Augustine *(below)* was a prime attraction during the height of the tourist era in the late 1800s. Now preserved as part of the Castillo de San Marcos National Monument, the gate is today open only to foot traffic. (SPA)

THE "DISCOVERY" of St. Augustine in 1883 by Henry M. Flagler was to have more immediate impact upon the peninsula than did the landing of Pedro Menendez de Avila in 1565. Flagler began construction in 1886 of the renaissance style Ponce de Leon Hotel, above, the first of Florida's great resort hotels outside of Jacksonville. The wealthy flocked to the Ponce de Leon Hotel, not just for the sunshine and the atmosphere of America's oldest city, but to enjoy the continental food and services, and to display their stylish clothes—like the beautiful people below in the Ponce de Leon's courtyard. (SPA)

PURCHASING the Ormond Hotel, at Ormond, in 1890, Flagler added two wings and a golf course. And, to improve transportation from Jacksonville to St. Augustine and to Ormond, he purchased the local railroads—a major step in the development of the East Coast. (SPA)

PARTNER of John D. Rockefeller in the founding of the Standard Oil Company, Henry M. Flagler began a second career in Florida in the 1880s—the building of the Flagler System, which was to occupy him until his death in 1913. (Miami Herald)

FEW RELICS REMAIN of the lively steamboat era when the picturesque St. Johns River was the number one tourist attraction in America. The ostentatious hotels and most of the homes built by winter residents have decayed, but a few charming little churches remain—at Orange Park, Hibernia, Green Cove Springs, Palatka. The Episcopal Church of Our Savior *(above)*, built at Mandarin in the early 1880s with help from Harriet Beecher Stowe, was flattened in 1965 when Hurricane Dora toppled a tree on it. But St. Mary's Episcopal *(below)* still stands at Green Cove Springs, as does St. Margaret's Episcopal *(right)* postage stamp-size church at Hibernia. (SPA—Miami Herald)

75

SURVIVING the hazards of time, these brick buildings still stand on Monroe Street in Tallahassee, although erected nearly a century ago. Both photographs were made in the 1880s. The store of E.H. Alford, above, is still operated under the name with a slight change—"Alford Brothers." "The Leon" saloon *(below)* went out of business with the passage of the Prohibition Act in 1920. Bennett's Drug Store now occupies the building. (SPA)

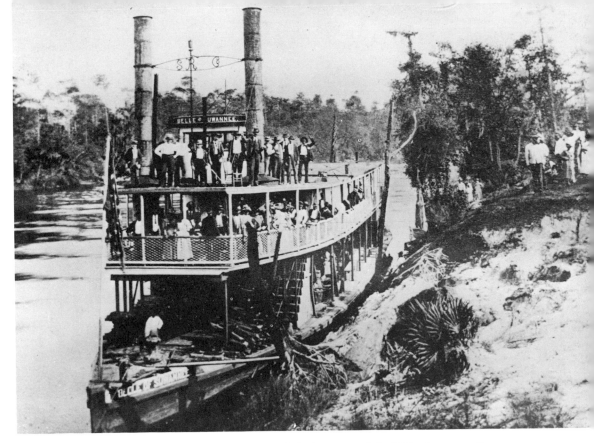

RIVERS provided the major travel routes in Florida until the latter part of the 1880s when expanding railroads began taking traffic away from the steamboats. Above, the whistle of the *Belle of Suwannee* brings people to the riverside at a landing near Branford. This steamboat was a favorite of honeymooning couples. Below, the *Rebecca Everingham* cuts the water of the Apalachicola River, laden with passengers and freight. (SPA)

OTHER AREAS in Florida were growing as well as the
northeastern section in the 1880s. Key West *(above)*, with
a surge in cigar manufacture, as well as in the sponge industry and shipping, grew from 10,000 in 1880 to 18,000
in 1890, edging out Jacksonville as Florida's largest city.
Pensacola *(below)* was a booming port in 1885, its exports being principally lumber, cotton, brick, and naval
stores. (SPA)

78

BUILT in 1878 and later expanded, the Convent of Mary Immaculate was, for three-fourths of a century, one of Key West's architectural gems. It was built by the Sisters of the Holy Names of Jesus and Mary, a Canadian Catholic organization. The Sisters served in the dual roles of teachers and nurses, and several of them lost their lives while nursing yellow fever victims during an epidemic in 1898. The building was razed in 1967 to make way for the Mary Immaculate High School. (SPA)

NO BEAUTY, like the Convent of Mary Immaculate in Key West, Bartow's first city hall and fire station was completely practical. The upper floor served as city hall, the first floor housed the hand-drawn fire-fighting equipment, including a ladder. Cost of the building, including the belfry for the fire alarm bell, was $685. Twenty-three members of the twenty-six member volunteer fire department appeared in July, 1887, for this photograph. (PCD)

EVERY FLORIDA community with cultural aspirations had an opera house in the late 1800s, but hardly any matched the Opera House at Pensacola. Built in 1883, it was knocked down in 1917, going the way of many of Florida's architectural treasures. (SPA)

LIVERY STABLE architecture in the 1800s included a hayloft and a vent on top to insure air circulation. Note the timber protruding from the wall above the door in the upper story. This was used for lifting bales of hay, with a rope slung over it. The photograph was made at Hawthorne about 1883. We even have the names of the four gentlemen: Toby Stock, Richard Smith, Elliot Watts, and Newt Coleman, but regret that the horses aren't identified. (SPA)

ROADS were little more than trails in the 1800s, and for a long time in the early 1900s—like the pineland road at left. Oxen *(below)* were the principal beasts of burden for heavy hauling, because horses and mules tended to bog down on muddy roads while cloven-hoofed, short-legged animals got through with ease. (SPA)

HORSEBACK was the fastest way to travel, next to train or steamboat. The cow pony, like these animals, was a special breed whose ancestry could be traced to Spanish times. These cowboys, wearing handguns, were Gainesville residents, Archie L. Jackson, left, and Thomas McDonald. When this photograph was made in the 1890s they had just driven a herd of cattle from Old Town, in Dixie County, to Gainesville, swimming them across the Suwannee. (SPA)

RIVER BRIDGES were virtually non-existent in Florida before the turn of the century. Crossings were made on ferries, like Irvine's Ferry on the Suwannee at Luraville in 1881. (SPA)

RURAL communities, like Monticello, seat of Jefferson County, may have been picturesque in their pastoral settings, and life simple, but, with the low status of medical knowledge life expectancy was short. There were no state-supported public schools, and most blacks and poor whites were lucky to learn how to read and write. Life revolved around the courthouse, where the lawyers, the most educated in the community, held sway. Monticello in 1885 had seven churches, all Protestant—four for whites and three for blacks. Jefferson County produced a number of influential political leaders, whose voices were important at Tallahassee. (SPA)

A LAWYER, businessman, banker, or physician could have owned this Tallahassee home in the 1880s, almost hidden behind foliage in a nearly forest-like setting. A black man has hitched the family horse to the buggy and stands waiting, probably for the master of the house, while the wife, dressed to go out, holds up her infant in its long dress for a man on horseback to admire. Note the absence of grass during an era when lawns were swept, not mowed. (SPA)

PORT CITIES, while less isolated than rural areas, were more subject to epidemics, like yellow fever which hit virtually all important Florida ports at one time or another during the 1800s. Although the epidemics were brought by ships, the transmission of the disease by mosquito would not be discovered until after the turn of the century. In the above drawing fires are being burned in Bay Street, Jacksonville, to destroy "fever germs." The gentlemen in the foreground are physicians. (SPA)

TYPICAL living room in the 1880s in northwest Florida, with an aged couple reading by the light of a kerosene lamp—this lamp, incidentally, much superior to those in most households at the time. Both use rocking chairs, while the bearded gentleman, evidently a tobacco chewer, has a spittoon on the floor at his left. The pictures on the mantel are of children and grandchildren. Although the man holds a cane, the couple may not be as old as they appear. Hard work, poor nutrition, and frequent contact with disease caused most persons to age early. "Rheumatism" was a common complaint among those fortunate to live past fifty. (SPA)

TRANSPORTATION by water was so important in the agricultural back country of Alachua County in the 1870s that a canal was dredged from Waldo, an important train stop, to Lake Santa Fe, by way of Lake Alto, in order to make fast delivery of oranges grown around Melrose. Alachua was a major citrus county, while Melrose was among the leading citrus centers in the state, until the winter of 1894-95 when freezes wiped out most of the groves of north Florida. Steamboats, like the *I.B. Lewis,* below, continued to use the Waldo Canal until the 1920s, when they could no longer compete with the motor vehicle after highways were improved. (SPA)

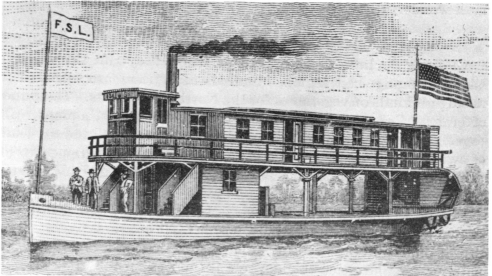

A STEREOSCOPIC craze which swept the nation during the latter decades of the 1800s sent photographers to virtually every spot of interest in search of subjects suitable for supplying the demand for the twin pictures by stereoscope owners. We owe a lot to these photographers, who recorded scenes and places which otherwise would have gone unphotographed. The curved top of the picture of the dredge *(above)* gives it away as having been engraved from a stereoscopic photograph. A number of other illustrations in this book were recorded by stereoscopic photographers. (SPA)

TO GRIND sugarcane, a mule was hitched to a long shaft that turned iron rollers as the animal walked round and round. The cane was fed through the rollers and the juice from the pressed stalks was collected in a tub. Virtually every farmer had a patch of sugarcane in the 1800s, which provided both syrup and brown sugar. Sugar was produced merely by cooking the cane juice until it was sufficiently evaporated to crystalize. (SPA)

CANE GRINDING was more than an industry; it was a time for socializing in the evening as families and neighbors gathered about the boiler in which the cane juice was "biled down" to syrup. As the juice boiled a person stood by with a small bucket attached to the end of long handle, and with this he skimmed off the foam and foreign matter that cooked to the top. The skimmings, dumped into a barrel, were fed to the hogs. If left long enough to ferment, the skimmings turned into potent "buck," which made pigs squeal in drunken delight. Or, the buck could be 'stilled into a potent white lightning of the kind that left a monstrous headache. (SPA)

GENERAL MERCHANDISE stores were located in every small town, like the one above, owned by R. B. Laffitte in Lloyd, near Tallahassee, in the late 1800s. The Laffitte family lived in the house at right. Below, the Cash Mercantile Company store at Wellborn, near Lake City, carried virtually everything—food, hardware, household things, dry goods, and garden seeds. Left to right are A.D. Hemming, Paul Hemming, and Elmer Mosely. (SPA)

THE METHODIST CHURCH at Bronson was built in 1886, when the Levy County community was a thriving center of citrus production. Among the signers of the charter was Dr. James M. Jackson, Sr., father of Dr. James M. Jackson, Jr., for whom Miami's Jackson Memorial Hospital is named. Dr. Jackson, Jr., moved to Miami in early 1896 after the 1894-95 freezes had wiped out the citrus of north Florida.

TELEGRAPH STATION at Punta Rassa, in Lee County, where the news of the sinking of the *U.S.S. Maine* was received by cable in 1898 and transmitted to the rest of the nation. The cable was laid in 1866 by the Inter-Ocean Telegraph Company, which strung telegraph wires to Jacksonville to connect with trunk lines. The building, on stilts, had been used as a barracks by soldiers during the Seminole Wars and by Union soldiers during the Civil War. It became known as the Shultz House after the Civil War, named for George R. Shultz, the telegrapher, who also operated the place as a make-shift hotel for cowboys. Jacob Summerlin drove thousands of cattle from central Florida to Punta Rassa in the 1860s and 1870s, from where they were shipped to Cuba. The chute through which cattle were driven onto the dock and into a waiting vessel may be seen below the elevated walk. A new telegraph office was built after the building was destroyed by the 1910 hurricane, but was abandoned in 1936 when the cable was extended to Fort Myers. (SPA)

FIRST MAJOR EFFORT to drain the swamp lands of Florida was made in the early 1880s by Hamilton Disston, who opened the Kissimmee Valley to development. Kissimmee was founded in 1882, and St. Cloud in 1887. Above is the Disston sugar mill at St. Cloud, while below is Kissimmee as it was in the late 1880s. Cowboys rode into town on Saturday night and "shot up" the place, but generally in a harmless way, firing into the air. Like Arcadia, Kissimmee had a horseman's saloon, where a man on horseback could order a whisky and drink it without dismounting. Jimmy Cowart's Bar in Kissimmee had such a setup until after World War II. (SPA)

AT FIRST GLANCE the City Bank of Kissimmee, built in the 1880s, resembles a Swiss chalet. Lake Tohokepaliga is in the background. (SPA)

BELIEVING his efforts to drain and develop the Kissimmee Valley had been a failure, and, facing bankruptcy, Hamilton Disston in 1893 shot himself. While his efforts to drain Lake Okeechobee had failed, some of Florida's finest cattle ranches were to be developed in the drained areas about Kissimmee in the early 1900s. (SPA)

FLAT-TOPPED straw hats and "shoe-laced" shirts were in style during the late 1800s when this photograph was made at Tallahassee. The gentleman in the center with handle-bar mustache and two-toned shoes is Captain Louis H. Strumm, while far right is Laurie A. Perkins. The man at left is unidentified. (SPA)

BUGGY decorated with roses won first place in the Live Oak floral show in 1900 for Mrs. Bessie Airth, left, and Mrs. Eva Hildreth. Below, a pair of mules draws a two-seated rig, and, with suitcases stashed behind the rear seat, it appears that somebody was planning a trip, by train or by steamboat. The photographer forgot to remove his carrying box from view when he shot this picture, sometime in the 1880s. (SPA)

LONG SHIRT and pants were in vogue for Old Tallahassee, veteran of the Seminole Indian wars. Chief Tallahassee and his Cow Creek followers lived on Catfish Lake, near the present Lake Wales. This photograph probably was made in Fort Myers. (SPA)

I'LL PUNCH you in the nose, this well-fed urchin seems to be saying. We don't know his name, but this child, of Hawthorne, would be in his nineties if living in 1974. (SPA)

MORE STYLES of the late 1800s, in Tallahassee. These people are unidentified, except for the young woman in the broad-brimmed hat decorated with bird plumes. She is Fanny Gibbons, a gorgeous blonde. We do know the name of the photographer who made the shot of the tense couple below—W.N. Kinsley of Tennessee. The gentleman is sitting on the photographer's carrying case, on which his name is scratched. (SPA)

LEGENDARY cowpoke of the prairies and palmetto woods about Arcadia, Morgan Bonapart (Bone) Mizell, is believed to have been used by Frederic Remington as the model for the painting at left done at Arcadia in the early 1890s for *Harper's Monthly*. The tintype of Mizell *(below)* was made in 1890 when he was twenty-seven. (PRVHS)

BONE MIZELL, although illiterate, was noted for his quick and cutting wit, developed as a result of having to counter mockery because of a lisp. Those who exchanged barbs with him invariably came off second best. Frequently in trouble because of his drinking, he was once asked by a judge how long it had been since his last drunk. "A momph," lisped Mizell. When the judge asked him what a "momph" was, Mizell shot back: "Hang hit, jedge, I tought ever'body knowed what a momph is—hit's firty days." Top "cow hunter" for Ziba King, Mizell kept books in his head. To pay off cowboys working for him, he withdrew funds from an Arcadia bank with a blank check signed by King, which the teller filled in. After he was found dead in the Fort Ogden railway depot on July 14, 1921, a physician listed the cause of death on a death certificate as "Moonshine—went to sleep and did not wake up." (Miami Herald)

ANOTHER LEGENDARY character of the Peace River Valley was James Mitchell (Acrefoot) Johnson, a long-legged, six-foot seven-inch walking mail man. Between 1877 and 1884 Acrefoot delivered mail once a week between Fort Ogden and Fort Meade, by way of Joshua Creek, Long Point, Gumheads, Bark Cowpens, Crewsville, and Berrach, making the sixty-five-mile route in one day. (PRVHS)

REMINGTON caught the perfect conformation of the tough and sprightly cattle pony in this painting of two Florida cowhands at Arcadia in the 1890s.

MAIN STREET, Arcadia, in the 1890s, when Bone Mizell and other cowpokes came into town on Saturday night to "live it up." A fire in 1904 burned these wood buildings.

MORALS WERE STRICT and permissiveness unheard of in 1885 when Albert Carlton—the bearded man with his family below—built this home in an orange grove near Wauchula, in the Peace River valley. With nine sons and one daughter, the Carltons turned most of the second floor into a boys' dormitory, reached by stairs between the porches. At one end of the second floor was the bedroom of the Carltons' daughter, Ella. Her room could be reached only by a stairway in her parents' first-floor bedroom. The old Carlton home still stood in 1974, occupied by a family employed in the Carlton groves.

STERN, religious, and disciplinarian were the Reverend William Penn McEwen and the former Ruth Strickland, parents of Martha McEwen Carlton, mother of the flock below. Virtually all the Carltons who inherited Ruth Strickland's genes would resemble her, including Doyle Carlton, Sr., Florida governor in 1929-33, and Doyle Carlton, Jr., unsuccessful candidate for governor in 1960. This tintype of the McEwens, who lived near Wauchula, was made in the 1880s. (PRVHS)

ALBERT AND MARTHA CARLTON pose with eight of their nine sons and daughter, Ella. Hard working and frugal, Albert and Martha built a rare kind of dynasty for their offspring—confidence, tenacity, spirit, and drive—and all made good in whatever field they ventured—cattle, citrus, banking, politics, law, medicine. The future governor of Florida, Doyle, is the serious boy in striped suit and boots, standing at the left of his mother. One son of Albert and Martha Carlton survived in 1974—Leffie, 77. He was yet to be born when this photograph was made in the 1890s. (Underwood)

A CUPOLA was added to the Florida State Capitol in 1891. Florida was growing and the increasing number of lawmakers, as well as administrative functions of the governor's office, required more space. But all the expansion the building got was the cupola. Another decade would pass before the needed expansion was started. (SPA)

THIS RUGGED GROUP from every part of Florida made up the 1889 State Senate. No, the well groomed lady in the front row was not a member, for it was not a time for women to be in politics, especially in the South. Eighteen of the figures wore beards, not counting the mustaches. Note the two-foot-long beard of the man in the second chair from left. Probably most of these men were lawyers, with businessmen second, but a few, like Ziba King of Arcadia and F. A. Hendry of Fort Myers, were cattlemen. No one is specifically identified in this photograph. (SPA)

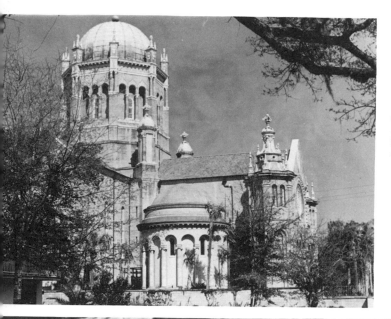

ST. AUGUSTINE got this magnificent Flagler Memorial Presbyterian Church in 1890, which the oil magnate erected in memory of his daughter, Jennie Louise, who died in 1889. The architects were Carrere & Hastings, who had designed the Ponce de Leon Hotel. Flagler was buried in a family tomb adjoining the church after his death in 1913.

THE YEAR 1892 is an important one for Florida because Flagler began that year to extend the Florida East Coast Railway south from Daytona. Only a few hardy pioneers lived in the area of Lake Worth and Biscayne Bay. Benjamin Lainhart, who had settled in Palm Beach in 1876, lived at first in the palmetto shack above—palmetto being the most convenient building material available. But in 1893 Flagler began building the Royal Poinciana Hotel *(left)* and southeast Florida would never be the same again. (SPA)

THE CREAM of society, industry, and finance flocked to Palm Beach in January, February, and March, traveling in private railway cars which were delivered over a bridge across Lake Worth virtually to the entrance of the Royal Poinciana Hotel. In the above photograph, made March 14, 1896, are Colonel Philip M. Lydig, Miss Helen Morton, Miss Gladys Vanderbilt, Miss Amy Townsend, Captain Rose, Mrs. Cornelius Vanderbilt, Miss Edith Bishop, Miss Mabel Gerry, Thomas Cushing, Edward Livingston, Dudley Winthrop, Craig Wadsworth, Gertrude Vanderbilt, Lispenard Stewart, Harry Payne Whitney, Miss Sybil Sherman, and Cornelius Vanderbilt. Gladys Vanderbilt, the last of this group to survive, became Countess Laszlo Szechenyi, wife of the envoy extraordinary and minister plenipotentiary to the United States from Hungary. She died in 1968. (PBCHS)

HATS were the fashion for men and women when this photograph was made on the piazza of the Royal Poinciana Hotel in the early days after its opening. (SPA)

THE TAMPA BAY Hotel was built in
1891 by Henry B. Plant, railroad devel-
oper, who wasn't about to be outdone by
Flagler's Ponce de Leon at St. Augustine.
Where Flagler had adapted the Spanish
Renaissance in his hotel design, Plant
turned to Cordova, Granada, and Mecca
in search of even greater extravagance.
Below is the front porch, above the
Moslem-like "minarets" which gave the
hotel the appearance of a super-mosque.
Never a money-maker, the hotel was taken
over in 1933 by the University of Tamapa.
(SPA)

HENRY B. PLANT, a Connecticut
Yankee, took the fortune he had made in
the express business after the Civil War
and built a network of railroads connecting Savannah, Jacksonville, and Tampa.
(SPA)

101

TROPICAL Biscayne Bay, translucent and abounding in fish and seaturtles, was discovered in the 1870s as an idyllic place by a few adventurers who were determined to live here. By 1886 the Bay had been discovered by a slightly larger number of Northerners who were equally determined to spend the winters here. The Peacock Inn at Coconut Grove was the Bay's first hotel. Here the Charles Peacocks hold a Christmas party in 1886 for "everybody living on Biscayne Bay." The Inn was expanded in succeeding years. (Merrick)

COCONUT GROVE'S winter residents during the winter of 1886-87 looked little different from the bearded people seen milling through the streets of the "Village" in the 1970s. They are, sitting, left to right: Kirk Munroe (a well known author), Count Jean d'Hedouville (of France), Alfred Munroe; middle: Dr. Tiger (Seminole medicine man), Ralph M. Munroe, Mrs. E. P. Brown, Miss Brown, Charles E. Stowe, Thomas A. Hine, Count James L. Nugent (of France), and E. P. Brown; top: Mrs. Thomas Munroe, Miss Flora McFarlane, Mrs. Kirk Munroe (who always turned her head from photographers), Edward A. Hine, and Mrs. Thomas A. Hine. To reach Coconut Grove, these residents took a steamer from New York to Key West and sailed through the Florida Keys to Biscayne Bay. (Miami Herald)

STARCH MAKING from coontie root, produced by a fern-like plant of the cycad family, offered most permanent residents of the Biscayne Bay area the only source of cash income before Flagler extended his railroad to Miami. In a mill like the one above, on the outskirts of Coconut Grove, one person could produce thirty to forty pounds of starch a day, which brought three to five cents a pound in Key West. (Merrick)

OLDEST RESIDENCE in the Miami area is the Barnacle, built on the Coconut Grove waterfront in 1891 by Commodore Ralph Munroe. In 1908 Munroe, needing a larger house, jacked up the bungalow and built a first floor beneath it. The house is now owned by the State of Florida. This photograph was made in the 1890s by Munroe.

FORT DALLAS, as it was in the 1880s, with author Kirk Munroe petting a yellow tabby cat. The building was moved to Miami's Lummus Park in 1925 to make way for a high-rise hotel, the Robert Clay. The hotel was razed in 1967 to make way for further development. (Miami Herald)

103

TWO DISASTROUS FREEZES hit Florida in the winter of 1894-95, killing 90 percent of the citrus. Groves like the one above, in north Florida, were killed to the ground. Florida had not suffered such a devastating freeze since 1835. In the meantime thousands of acres of citrus had been planted farther and farther north in the peninsula, and huge trees, like the one below, thrived. This one, promoted as the "largest orange tree in Florida," grew near Waldo in Alachua County. It bore as many as 10,000 oranges a year in the 1880s. Like nearly all the other citrus trees in north Florida, it was killed in the 1894-95 freezes. The effect of the freezes on the state was staggering, and no other event in Florida's history, except its becoming a United States possession in 1821, has resulted in so many changes. (SPA)

THE FREEZES failed to reach Miami, then a community of three or four houses near the mouth of the Miami River. Among the residents was Mrs. Julia Tuttle, a widow with two children. She had purchased Fort Dallas, below, started in the 1840s as a plantation house and slave quarters, but abandoned, to be completed by the military during the Seminole War of 1855-58. Mrs. Tuttle purchased the buildings, together with a square mile of property, and moved here from Cleveland in 1891 with her children and a milk cow. She remodeled the structures, adding the columns and fake dormer to the one-story building. This building had served as the Dade County courthouse before 1889, when the county seat was moved to Juno, on Lake Worth. After the February freeze of 1895 Mrs. Tuttle snipped from an orange tree in her garden a green twig with white blooms and sent it to Flagler in St. Augustine, together with an invitation to extend his railroad from West Palm Beach to Biscayne Bay. Flagler decided in June, 1895, to extend his railroad to Miami, to lay out a community, and build a resort hotel. (SPA)

THE FIRST TRAIN arrived in Miami on April 22, 1896, but more than a thousand persons already had flocked to the promising new place, having abandoned frozen groves or left communities that were being deserted after the freezes. By June, 3,000 were counted in Miami, but most must have considered themselves temporary residents, because only 502 turned out on July 28 to vote for Miami's incorporation. The unidentified family *(left)* planned permanent residence, having built this house in the vicinity of Northeast First Street near Second Avenue. The photograph of the train was made the day after its arrival. (Miami-Metro—SPA)

MIAMI'S ROYAL PALM Hotel, with 400 rooms and suites, opened January 16, 1897. But the first visitors, John Jacob Astor and his son, Vincent, arrived just before Christmas, 1896, three weeks before the hotel's completion. While the Astors fished in Biscayne Bay with guide Charlie Thompson, hotel employees set up a Christmas tree in the lobby. A clerk would remember young Vincent appearing on Christmas morning in a white sailor suit, happy to discover that Santa Claus got as far south as Miami. John Jacob Astor was to lose his life in the sinking of the *Titanic,* while Vincent would visit Miami on his yacht *Nourmahal,* with President Franklin D. Roosevelt as his guest. (Miami Herald)

MIAMI'S FIRST RAILWAY station was built at Northeast Sixth Street and present Biscayne Boulevard, near Flagler's P. & O. Steamship docks. The entrance was designed for horse carriages, before the first motor cars were seen in Miami. A larger station was built in 1912, a block north of the Dade County Courthouse. (Miami Herald)

THE MANY-GABLED Belleview Hotel, built at Belleair by Henry B.
Plant, opened on January 15, 1897, beating the opening of Flagler's
Royal Palm in Miami by one day. Wealthy guests came in their private
railway cars, delivered to the hotel entrance. The hotel's two cham-
pionship golf courses were its principal attraction, but the rough tee
(*right*) would hardly be attractive today when golf turfs are maintained
in elegant condition. The Belleview is still in operation, and its golf
courses have no rough tees. (Dunn)

108

TAMPA became a major embarcation port during the Spanish-American War, as men, horses, and military equipment were shipped here for the invasion of Cuba in July, 1898. A strong nationalism spread across the country, and particularly in Florida where many feared an attack by the Spanish fleet. Parades

110

like this one down Tampa's Franklin Street in the spring of 1898 were held in other Florida cities to demonstrate support of the war against Spain and the will to put up a determined defense if attacked. (Dunn)

HORSES AND TROOPS at the Port of Tampa wait their turn to be loaded onto transports for the invasion of Cuba and Puerto Rico in the summer of 1898. (SPA)

SAME OLD army game is recognizable in this 1898 camp at Tampa, with the armed soldier walking his post "in a military manner," while a bugler blows one of the innumerable calls heard through the day between reveille and taps. The bugler stands beside the first of a string of two-man "pup" tents. The larger tent at right, with cots and mattresses, is for officers. (SPA)

THEODORE ROOSEVELT on the beautiful star-blazed horse which carried him up San Juan Hill, and, figuratively, into the White House. Elected governor of New York four months later, Roosevelt was drafted for vice-president in 1900, and succeeded the assassinated President McKinley in 1901. He'd hardly had time to get out of the saddle since San Juan. (Dunn)

COLONEL ROOSEVELT at the head of his Rough Riders, just before embarking at Tampa for Cuba and the attack on San Juan in July. (SPA)

SNOW FELL in Tallahassee in February, 1899—enough for a snowball battle on the steps of the Capitol. (SPA)

*Opposite page:* AN IMPOSING DOME was added to the State Capitol in 1902, in keeping with Florida's bolstered pride over the role it had played in the recent easy victory over Spain. The dome replaced a humble and architecturally disproportionate cupola, stuck on top of the building in 1891. North and south wings were also added in 1902. (SPA)

# *Florida from 1900 to World War I*

TRAINS AND HORSES predominated at the turn of the century for long-distance and short-distance travel. As train time approached a community's activities began to concentrate at the depot, as at the Seaboard Air Line station in Ocala *(above)*. Although the motor car had made its appearance in a few places, it was rarely seen in the back country of Florida, where good roads were non-existent. At center is the Florida East Coast Railway depot at New Smyrna, below the Atlantic Coast Line depot at Bartow. (SPA)

STEAMBOAT traffic had been hurt by the expansion of the railroads, but a few boats still managed to operate in the 1900s, like the *City of Jacksonville (above)* on the St. Johns River at Jacksonville, and *Three States (below)* at Branford on the Suwannee River. Steamboats would be eventually put out of business by the automobile and the building of modern highways. (SPA)

A CARELESSLY TOSSED match or cigarette in a mattress factory ignited a fire on the morning of May 3, 1901, which leveled 130 blocks of Jacksonville. By the morning of May 4, when the above photograph was made from atop the Federal Building, most of the city was in ashes, including the luxury hotels. Below, soldiers patrol after the fire, at Main and Bay streets. The tower of the Federal Building, which survived the fire, may be seen at right. (SPA)

JACKSONVILLE'S comeback after the fire was rapid. Above is the new Windsor Hotel, replacing the famous hostelry built during the era when Jacksonville was the tourist capital of Florida. This photograph was made in 1903, looking northwest across Hemming Park. Below, Forsyth Street in 1905. Automobiles are beginning to make their appearance in increasing numbers. (SPA)

ONCE there were three bears—in Jacksonville—and they climbed telephone poles, walked about on their hind legs with the aid of sticks, and did such tricks as turning "somersets" for the amusement of bystanders who were asked to contribute pennies and nickels. This picture was made by a stereoscopic photographer on the lookout for scenes and subjects that would sell stereo mounts. (SPA)

BASEBALL was a popular sport in rural communities, where, as in Gainesville *(above)*, members of a well-to-do family turned out in a surrey drawn by a "double team" to root for their favorite side. (SPA)

GOLF was a society sport in 1905, when players dressed in their Sunday best before going out to the links. Note the "green" on this course at DeLand is not green at all but consists of leveled, smoothed, and packed earth about the cup. (SPA)

THE WIDE BEACH at Ormond and Daytona
became the world's best known automobile
testing ground in the early 1900s, and the plush
Ormond Hotel *(right)* was the drivers' headquarters. Barney Oldfield, Ralph De Palma, and
William K. Vanderbilt, Jr., consistently set new
records and broke them. Henry Ford came down
in the winter of 1904 to demonstrate his flivver,
but, lacking the price of a hotel room, slept in his
car. Below, a beach scene at Daytona in 1904.
Note that the horses are paying no attention to
the noisy motorized buggy proceeding along the
beach, indicating that they are accustomed to the
obstreperous machines without visible horsepower. (SPA)

YOU HAD A CHOICE in "coaching" at
the Hotel Ormond—in a horse-drawn
vehicle or in a vehicle operated by the
horsepower of an internal combustion
engine. Note the height of the seats above
the ground. That was for fording streams
in the days before bridges and culverts
were universal. (SPA)

SIGHTSEEING trips up the beautiful Tomoka River was a must for guests at the Hotel Ormond. And there was always a sportsman with a gun standing in the bow, to shoot at everything that took to the air and every animal that showed its head, including alligators. At the moment the sportsman is interested in the young women, venturing out "on a limb" over the quiet river. The *Nemo* was steam-powered. (SPA)

SAILING on the beach was great sport at Ormond in 1903. In the distance are pedal-operated wheel chairs, called Afromobiles because blacks usually furnished the pedal-power. (SPA)

BEACH STREET, Daytona, in 1906, below. Look at those telephone poles, with twelve arms, each carrying ten wires. How would you like to have been a lineman then? (SPA)

CENTRAL AVENUE, now St. Petersburg's main street, underwent considerable change during the period between 1895, when the above photograph was made, and 1901 when the shot below was taken. For one thing, the street had been paved. The community had been founded in 1888 by Peter Demens, builder of the Orange Belt Railroad, who named the place in honor of his native St. Petersburg, Russia, now Leningrad. (Dunn—SPA)

123

CELEBRATION of George Washington's birthday was society's major event in Florida—like this party at the home of E. M. Belsford, One South Lake Trail, on February 22, 1905. The children were invited, too, and you can bet there was no misbehaving in that strict era. (SPA)

THE BEACH CLUB, most famous gambling house to operate in the Unitd States, was opened in 1898 by Colonel E. R. Bradley, native of Johnstown, Pennsylvania. The sports lion of his age, he became known as the highest-stake gambler in history. So influential and astute was Bradley that the club operated every winter until his death in 1946 without molestation. Bradley's will provided that upon his death the club was to be razed, the gambling equipment towed out to sea and sunk, and the land given to Palm Beach as a park. A historic plaque in a greensward on Poinciana Way marks the site. (PBCHS)

THE BREAKERS, Flagler's beach-front hotel (above) at Palm Beach, was built in 1896 as The Inn. It became The Breakers in 1900, but burned in a spectacular fire in 1903. A second Breakers began rising as soon as the ashes cooled, but it, too, was to be a victim of fire, burning on March 18, 1925, in a conflagration (below) no less spectacular than the one in 1903. A third Breakers, more opulently planned than its predecessors, was opened in 1926. It is still in operation. (SPA—PBCHS)

KORESHAN UNITY, a religious sect whose members practiced celibacy and believed they lived inside the globe, established a communal colony at Estero, near Fort Myers, in 1894. The sexes, parents as well as children, lived in separate dormitories. The first men's dormitory *(left)* was of logs, with thatched roof. (Michel)

SEXES MIXED in the dining hall, at concerts, religious services, sports, and outings, such as one getting under way *(above)* in front of the first store at Estero. The early Model T Fords suggest a period about 1910. The road is now Highway 41.

CYRUS TEED, a Chicago physician, conceived Koreshan Universality, a mixture of Judeo-Christian thought, mysticism, and science. He believed thought was indestructible, but that only through celibacy could the human reach perfection. Teed planned a city of ten million at Estero, which he called New Jerusalem.

BREAD WAS BAKED for some 200 members of Koreshan Unity in the early days at Estero. To become members it was necessary to give up worldly possessions to the Unity.

KORESHANS lived inside the globe, as this model demonstrates. The sun is the center of the universe, whose diameter is 8,000 miles rather than the infinite distance recognized by astronomers. This makes the sun only 4,000 miles from the earth's surface. The cut-away universe, showing the position of the sun, stars, and planets, is on exhibit in Art Hall, Koreshan State Park, Estero.

ART HALL and a few other buildings erected by members of Koreshan Unity still survive, but all the original members of the commune have passed on. In Art Hall is a collection of relics left behind by members, including musical instruments, and paintings by Douglas Arthur Teed, the founder's son.

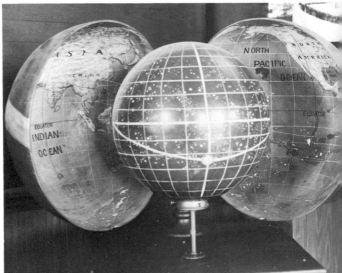

PORTS—Jacksonville, Tampa, Pensacola, and Key West—were Florida's largest cities in the early 1900s. Pensacola *(above)* owed much of its economic life to the export of timber. Left is the old L & N depot in Pensacola.

MIAMI *(below)* had fewer than 2,000 residents in 1900, but the population would reach 5,471 by 1910, ranking it sixth among Florida cities. Flagler Street was at first paved with white limestone. (Fishbaugh)

INTERIOR TOWNS grew at a slower rate after 1900 than they had grown in the 1800s. This 1906 street scene in Live Oak, seat of Suwannee County, would change little in the next half-century, except that pavement would replace the dirt surface, and the number of automobiles would increase. Live Oak was founded in 1866. (SPA)

SILVER SPRINGS had lost none of its charm, but steamboat travel up the Oklawaha was no longer as popular in the early 1900s as it had been during the late 1800s when the St. Johns River was a foremost tourist attraction. The winter touring crowd was now passing by Jacksonville in favor of Ormond, Palm Beach, and Miami. Destruction of the river's once abundant wildlife had much to do with the public's disenchantment, and now the timber was being cut along the Oklawaha and rafted downstream to sawmills at Palatka. Although a few did stop off in Jacksonville to make the river trip to Silver Springs, it was impossible to recapture the romance of a now departed era. (SPA)

TIMBER was one of Florida's major industries for half a century after the end of the Civil War—until the great forests were denuded. The scene above was multiplied many times in northwest and north Florida during the early 1900s. (SPA)

A STEAM CRANE *(below)* loads pine logs onto a flatcar. (SPA)

SAWMILLS like this one of the Calhoun Timber Company at Apalachicola reduced millions of Florida pine and cypress logs to lumber. (SJPC)

DURING THE HEIGHT of timber cutting in northeast Florida, Fernandina's port was busy with shipping operations. Much of the loading was done by hand (and back) labor. (SPA)

A NEW MANSION for the governor of Florida was erected at Tallahassee in 1906. Of Georgian-colonial style, it resembled the traditional Southern gentleman's plantation house. Governor Napoleon Bonaparte Broward moved into the mansion in 1907. It was demolished during the administration of Governor LeRoy Collins and replaced in 1957 by a new mansion which resembles Andrew Jackson's "Hermitage" near Nashville. The column on the drawn-out wagon *(below)* was made for the 1906 mansion. (SPA)

THE DIRTY DOZEN, Miami "rough-house gang," strikes a pose in the gardens of the Royal Palm Hotel. Each holds a cigar and each wears a hibiscus, probably plucked from the shrubs behind them. Only four of the nine are identified. They are, left to right, Robert E. Coates, third; Roddy Burdine, fifth; Jeff Gautier, seventh; and Freeman Burdine, ninth. Roddy was to grow up to head Burdine's Department Store and to have the Roddy Burdine Stadium (Orange Bowl) named for him. (HASF)

EVERY FLORIDA community had its Civil War veterans. These old soldiers of Company D, First Florida Reserve Regiment, Confederate States of America (C.S.A.) attended the state convention at Live Oak in 1909. They are, front row, left to right, John D. Willis, Robert Pickles, Joseph P. Webb, Arnett Landing; back row: John T. Clark, S. W. Page, Sylvanus Mortimer Hankins, and Andrew J. Loper. (SPA)

AN INGENIOUS LAD, Victor Grant-
ham, hitched his wagon to a star—a bull
calf—and rode down Main Street in
Sarasota in 1906 without creating any to-
do at all. But a rural atmosphere pre-
vailed even at the Belle Haven Inn *(below)* in downtown Sarasota, where the chickens were fed on the
hotel lawn. No objections were made to the chickens, but merchants objected to hogs wallowing in the
mud hole created by the overflow of a watering trough on Main Street and cattle herds roaming through
the town to graze the vacant lots. Mayor Hamden Smith led a bitter fight to get an ordinance passed
which prohibited farm animals the same freedom downtown that taxpayers enjoyed. (Marth)

134

TWO DUDES from Brown's Boat Landing, Seminole Josie Billie and Frank Brown, get themselves photographed in a Fort Myers studio and thereby became a part of Florida's pictorial history. They had made the sixty-five-mile journey in 1908 by ox cart. Brown's trading post was located on the border between Big Cypress Swamp and the Everglades, an important hub of canoe trails dating back before Columbus. The trails disappeared with drainage of the Everglades—and so did Brown's Landing. Frank Brown, growing up among the Indians, learned to speak the Indian language so well he was frequently used as an interpreter in court when non-English speaking Seminoles were called as witnesses. Josie and Frank were alive in 1974, both in their upper eighties. (Tebeau)

SEMINOLE INDIANS, in long shirts and wearing bowler hats, have just finished loading their dugouts with supplies bought at Frank Stranahan's trading post on New River at Fort Lauderdale, and are preparing to pole upstream and return to their Everglades haunts. They had sold Stranahan deer and otter skins, alligator hides, and bird plumes, and with the money bought food and ammunition, plus some wyome (whiskey) on the sly. It was at that time illegal to sell whiskey to an Indian.

135

NAVAL STORES, or turpentining, was an important industry before the petrochemical age. Long-leaf and slash pines were tapped by making "catfaces" on tree trunks (above), and the bleeding gum was caught in cups, or in boxes cut in the trees. Gum was then hauled to the distillery *(below)*. Here the turpentine was distilled from the gum. The residue, drained into barrels, hardened into rosin upon cooling. Some turpentining still goes on in Florida, but not to the extent as in the early 1900s. These scenes were in northwest Florida over half a century ago. (SPA)

PINEAPPLE growing was a major agricultural industry along the Florida East Coast in the early 1900s. This is the Zapf farm at Juno, above the shore of Lake Worth. The "pines" were shipped by train to northern cities. Competition from Cuba, plus insects and diseases, eventually wiped out the industry. (SPA)

FARMERS resorted to the most convenient kind of transportation in the early 1900s to market their products. A sailboat has brought a load of fresh vegetables and charcoal to Key West, probably from the Chokoloskee Bay country or from Flamingo. Charcoal, made from buttonwood, was in constant demand on an island which lacked fuel sources of its own. (SPA)

137

138    PHOSPHATE MINING had its beginning in Florida in 1888, in shallow mines where hand labor could be used to remove the mineral, like that at Dunnellon *(above)* in 1890. Then the steam shovel, like the one at Anthony, in Marion County, was introduced. The steam shovel not only could do the work of scores of men, but made it possible to remove phosphate from much deeper levels below the surface than was practical with the use of hand labor. (SPA)

DISCOVERY of rich phosphate deposits in Polk County brought major mining operations southward after the turn of the century and the building of large plants like the one (above) near Fort Meade. By World War II operations had expanded into plants like that *(below)* at Brewster. Huge drag lines worked round the clock removing deposits from as much as fifty feet below the surface. The world demand would grow to such astounding levels that by the 1970s Florida would be producing over 75 percent of the nation's rock phosphate and one-third of the world's output—more than 30 million tons valued at more than $150 million. (SPA)

KEY WEST at one time supplied 90 percent of the nation's sponges, but in 1905 Greek spongers, working out of Tarpon Springs (above), began using diving equipment to gather sponges rather than a pole and hooks. Within a short time a thousand Greek divers were sponging in the Gulf of Mexico, and the Tarpon Springs sponge market became the largest in the world. Enormous piles of sponges were loaded onto the docks when the sponge fleet came into port. (SPA)

MODERN DIVING equipment used by Greek sponge divers (left) made it possible for them to work at depths of 100 feet. Diseases eventually decimated sponge colonies at Tarpon Springs and Key West, but by that time inexpensive synthetic sponges were displacing the natural sponges on the market. (SPA)

LINEMEN for the old Peninsula Telephone Company in Tampa—now General Telephone Company—worked out of a wagon in 1906. If the mule looks a little old that's because young animals were never used for this kind of work, which required a lot of standing and waiting. An older animal has more patience than one that's young and heady. (SPA)

THE TELEGRAPH STATION and ticket office at Hawthorne was a rather dark place during the day time, and a kerosene lamp supplied the light at night. We don't have the gentleman's name, but he evidently served as passenger ticket agent, freight agent, express agent, and telegrapher. According to the Atlantic Coast Line calendar in the window it is January, 1912. Note the glass telegraph pole insulators on the chair legs. It permitted the agent to slip about easily from one job to another without rising. (SPA)

EARLY CARS varied enormously in style. Wouldn't you like to take a spin in this 1912 Oakland, owned by Mr. and Mrs. Cory S. Lefevre of Luraville? Its lights were Prest-O-Lite, developed by Carl Fisher who was to spend millions of dollars in the building of Miami Beach. Fisher promoted the building of the Dixie Highway between Florida, Indianapolis, and Chicago. (SPA)

FORERUNNER of Henry Ford's Model T was this specially built, extra wide Tin Lizzie, hand-made in 1907 for his friend, Thomas A. Edison. Edison wanted the car extra wide so that he could follow the ox-trail roads about the vicinity of Fort Myers, where he had established a winter home and laboratory in the 1880s. In 1909 Ford came out with his famous Model T, which "put America on wheels." Proud of his hand-made car, Edison refused Ford's offer of new assembly line models, as well as a new Lincoln after Ford acquired that company in 1922. Edison's old car, on exhibit at the Edison Winter Home museum in Fort Myers, is still in running condition. (Edison)

LOOKS LIKE a stand-off between a motor car and a double team of horses that encounter each other in front of the First National Bank of Miami. If you're an old car buff you'll have no trouble identifying the make and the year, and, if you're old enough, you'll identify the horse-drawn vehicle as a surrey. This first home of the First National Bank, built in the early part of the century, was at East Flagler Street and Northeast First Avenue. (SPA)

THE FLORIDA NATIONAL BANK

FLORIDA NAT'L BANK & BISBEE BLDG. B16820
Jacksonville, Fla.
Copyright 1910 By
IRVING UNDERHILL, New York.

CARS EXCEED the number of horses in this 1910 Jacksonville scene. This is the original home of the Florida National Bank chain. After the Florida National was acquired in the late 1920s by Alfred I. duPont it was expanded to thirty banks throughout Florida, to become one of the richest financial institutions in the South. (SPA)

THE THREE R's—reading, 'riting, and 'rithmetic—were frequently taught in a one-room school house before World War I, as was done in this Jacksonville school in 1910. One teacher usually had the impossible task of conducting classes from the primer through the sixth grade. In many back-country settlements the one-room school persisted until the 1930s, when the upheaval of the Great Depression brought about enormous social and economic changes in Florida. (SPA)

HOW DID THE KIDS get to school in the days before the motor bus? A mule-drawn wagon covered with canvas (*below*) provided the principal means in 1911 at West Palm Beach, but bicycles were coming into use, too. Note the boy and the girl carrying their lunch baskets hanging from the handlebars. A double-team of dray horses (*left*) is used to draw a "wagonette" in Duval County in 1898, according to the date on the photo. What appear to be automobile tire tracks in the foreground indicate a much later date. (SPA)

WITH A LAUREL OAK as a back rest, a student at Stetson University hits the books while other students peer from a third-story window of Stetson Hall. The year is 1904. Founded in 1883 as DeLand Academy, after the founder of the town and the school, Henry A. DeLand, the name was changed in 1899 as a reward to John B. Stetson, wealthy hat manufacturer, for his generous support. Florida's first law school was opened here in 1900. (SPA)

IT WAS WILD, man, when a University of Florida student (below) took his girl friend for a ride on his Indian motorcycle in 1914. A gal had to sit "side-saddle," because it was in the days of the ankle-length dress, before women wore stretch pants or dungarees. Members of I Ata Pie (right) at the Florida State College for Women in Tallahassee had their fun, too. The year is 1911, and the gals taking part in the annual pie-eating wing-ding are, in no special order, Constance Bishop, Mary Hall, Halley Ley, Eugenia Nolan, Joe Berta Bryan, Olive Petty, Ruby Hall, Bessie Eddy, and Winifred Pedrick. (SPA)

145

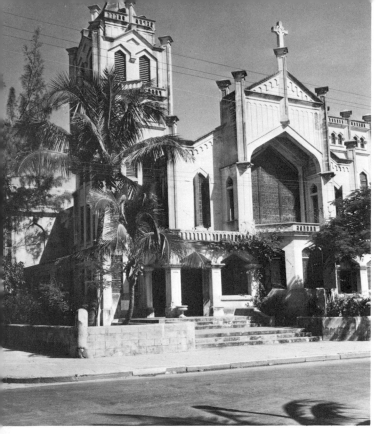

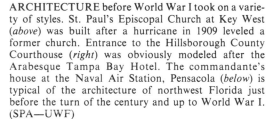

ARCHITECTURE before World War I took on a variety of styles. St. Paul's Episcopal Church at Key West (*above*) was built after a hurricane in 1909 leveled a former church. Entrance to the Hillsborough County Courthouse (*right*) was obviously modeled after the Arabesque Tampa Bay Hotel. The commandante's house at the Naval Air Station, Pensacola (*below*) is typical of the architecture of northwest Florida just before the turn of the century and up to World War I. (SPA—UWF)

GREAT HATS decorated with bows of silk were in style in 1912 when Mrs. Glenn D. Moore, Sr., of Hawthorne posed in the local photographic studio. A campaign by the National Audubon Society against the shooting of aquatic birds for their fancy plumes had done much to reach the conscience of American women, most of whom disdained the wearing of hats decorated at the expense of dead birds. Mrs. Moore's charm suffers none from the absence of plumes in her hat. (SPA)

BATHING STYLES at Miami Beach have changed a bit since 1910. Only the men could expose their knees, as the man at left is doing. It was at a time when few women could swim—and with good reason, when you consider the garb they had to wear. Note the "life line" in the middle distance and how few have ventured beyond it. (SPA)

A HISTORIC CELEBRATION at Pensacola occurred on December 18, 1911, when Governor Albert W. Gilchrist of Florida delivered a $10,000 silver service to the newly commissioned U.S. Battleship *Florida*. Funds for the purchase of the silver service were donated by Floridians, including children who gave pennies, nickels, and dimes. Returned to Florida after the battleship was decommissioned in 1931, the silver service is today in the governor's mansion in Tallahassee. (SPA)

NATIONAL GUARDSMEN were more visible in 1910 before the development of cities into metropolitan areas. Miami's National Guard unit, in marching order, stands attention in Flagler Street, in preparation for a parade to demonstrate its readiness. In the background is the old Dade County Courthouse, built in 1904. (SPA)

THIS RARE VIEW of the Everglades, with its saw grass prairies and tree islands, was made on January 29, 1912, from a sightseers' tower on Musa Isle, near the forks of the Miami River. The stream, at left, is the north fork of the river, while the big ditch at upper right is the Miami Canal. In the distance you may note a dam, or plug, in the canal, later removed upon completion of dredging operations. This dam is the approximate location of Northwest Thirty-Sixth Street and the Airport Interchange. Development of the Everglades began immediately after drainage, and today all of the area shown here is occupied by expanding Miami. Hialeah, upper right; Miami Springs, in the middle distance, and the northeast corner of Miami International Airport, at upper left. Drainage of the Everglades was begun in 1905 during the administration of Governor Napoleon Bonaparte Broward. With the opening of the canals the water in the Everglades dropped sharply. Idyllic scenes like the one above quickly disappeared, and by the 1970s a million people would live in an area that once had been the home of frogs, fish, and alligators. This photograph remained for years in the Library of Congress as an unidentified Everglades scene until discovered by Allen Morris, founder of the State Photographic Archives at Tallahasse. (SPA)

149

BRICKELL MANSION, Miami's finest early home, was located on the south side of Miami River, facing what is now Brickell Avenue. William and Maude Brickell built a trading post at the mouth of the river in the 1870s, and the family acquired some 700 acres of property, extending along Biscayne Bay to Coconut Grove. Brickell, the bearded man sitting in a chair, built a road from Miami through the jungle to Coconut Grove in 1892. He died in 1902 after being kicked in the head by a mule. The Brickell house, riddled by termites, was later dismantled. (SPA)

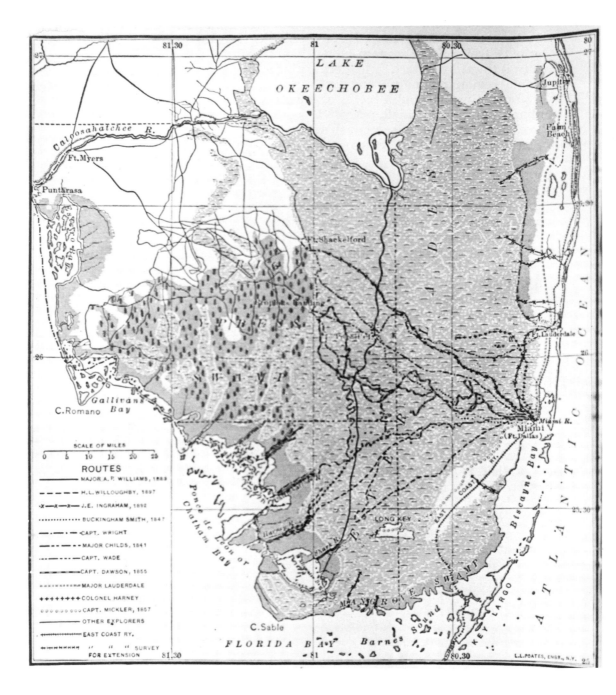

THE EVERGLADES was a mysterious wilderness in 1905 when the state began cutting drainage canals between Lake Okeechobee and tidewater at Miami, Fort Lauderdale, Deerfield, and West Palm Beach. This drawing depicts south Florida as it was in 1904, before Flagler had begun his Key West extension over the surveyed route south of Homestead, founded in October, 1904. The wiggly lines meandering about the Everglades are "trails" of explorers, and military expeditions in search of elusive Seminoles. Note the demarcation between the Everglades and Big Cypress Swamp, and also the numerous ox-cart roads in the upper part of the Swamp. Bill Brown operated a trading post at Brown's Boat Landing, near Fort Shackelford, but the map maker failed to include it. Homestead is not included because it was founded some months after the map was made. (SPA)

150

A VIEW from the *Suwanee*, at the familiar flat-topped cypress near the confluence of the Caloosahatchee and Lake Okeechobee. Looking from the same vantage point today you would see the town of Moore Haven and the bridge of U.S. 27 arching over the river. Lake Okeechobee you would not see, which was ensconced behind a levee after the 1926 hurricane drove a tide over Moore Haven, drowning between 200 and 300. (The levee was not built, however, until the 1928 hurricane drowned 2,000 on the south lake shore in one terrifying hour.) To reach the lake from the Caloosahatchee now you must go through a lock. Unbelievably, the cypress still stands—in a park where it shades picnicking tables. (SPA)

DOCKSIDE during the noon hour at Jacksonville in 1911, when a stevedore got ten cents an hour for ten hours work, and paid a dime for lunch prepared by women vendors. Living costs were cheap, there were no deductions for Social Security, insurance, union dues, the United Fund, or income tax. But a working man made too little to save anything. With nothing to look forward to but a rheumatoid, pensionless old age, most sought what little pleasure they could find at the moment, often spending their hard-earned wages for cheap whiskey. (SPA)

SIX DAYS a week and ten hours a day was the working schedule for just about everyone before World War I, but Sunday was a day for rest and simple pleasures—like canoeing on the Hillsborough River near Sulphur Springs. People dressed in their best to go to church, and in their second best for an outing. Fishing on Sunday was frowned upon as "breaking the Sabbath." (SPA)

NO WONDER Miami got on the map in those days; somebody was always pulling a hoax which got wide publicity, like von Moser, an unbathed German "nobleman" (far right), who reported he had captured the "largest python in the world" in Brickell Hammock, on the edge of downtown. Hundreds naively paid a dime to gawk at the snake while it gradually starved to death. A *Miami News* reporter revealed that von Moser had bought the snake from a New York zoo, and cheaply because it refused to eat. Zoo keepers had not learned that you could force-feed a snake.

BIGGEST PUBLICITY getter of them all was Miami's Captain Charlie Thompson (holding gaff), who in 1915 ignited a nationwide controversy after reporting he had found a human skull in the stomach of the leopard shark in the foreground, displayed on the Miami River waterfront. Earlier, Thompson claimed to have caught a 30,000-pound whale shark in the Florida Keys. Actually, the huge animal "landed" itself in shallow water. Thompson recovered the shark, had it mounted, and hauled the monster about the nation, charging admission to see it. (SPA)

DEVELOPMENT of the motor car brought pressure for the improvement of highways, but roads and bridges were costly and funds to build them were scarce. A one-way steel bridge was built across the Suwannee at Luraville in 1907, replacing a too-busy, too-slow, ferry. It would have to last for forty years. Paving was done mainly by hand labor, like the road in Polk County *(below)*, while convicts and mules *(left)* frequently were used to construct roads even as late as the 1920s. (SPA)

POOR ROADS may have slowed up the cautious driver but not the speed demon—except whenever he lost control in the winding ruts and flipped, as did this car in Alachua County, near Hawthorne. But six men could upright a car, and usually, if the driver was still alive, and sober, he could crank up and continue his way. (SPA)

A HIGHWAY OPENING was excuse for an all-out celebration, like the opening of a twenty-mile leg of the Dixie Highway between St. Augustine and Hastings in 1915. Carl Fisher, owner of Prest-O-Lite for automobiles, had promoted the Dixie Highway, from Chicago and Indianapolis to Florida, but long stretches would remain unpaved until the 1920s. (SPA)

155

VIZCAYA, modeled after an Italian nobleman's villa, with baroque gardens, was begun at Miami in 1914 by James Deering, wealthy farm equipment manufacturer. Miami was in the midst of a recession following the death of Flagler in 1913, but Deering, also a big spender, provided jobs for 1,000. Deering moved in at Christmas time, 1916, on the eve of World War I. Although the war would leave an immensely greater impact upon the development of the new city, Vizcaya set the ostentatious "Mediterranean" architectural style for Florida's boom years of the 1920s. The house and grounds are maintained today as a museum. (Hoit)

TRIUMVIRATE in invention, natural history, and manufacturing—Thomas A. Edison, John Burroughs, and Harvey Firestone—gather in the tropical garden of Edison's winter home at Fort Myers in 1914. They made collecting trips into Big Cypress Swamp, returning with orchids and other unusual plants. Or they might lease the steamer *Suwanee* for a trip up the Caloosahatchee to Lake Okeechobee. Henry Ford frequently made a fourth. (Edison)

CHULUOTA was the center of a major land development project in 1914, initiated by the Model Land Company, a Flagler System enterprise, to attract settlers to Florida and make business for the Florida East Coast Line Railway. Thousands of acres were cut up into ten-acre grove sites, but few came to buy. Meanwhile, a branch rail line was extended from New Smyrna to Okeechobee, where engineers made plans for a city larger than Miami. But that project failed, too. After the trains stopped running in the 1930s, the track was taken up and the depots sold.

A COMMUNITY friendship was shared by Floridians before World War I that resulted in fish frys, camp meetings, or Sunday dinners-on-the-ground, usually sponsored by churches, which provided a center of social activity. The meeting *(below)* at Floridatown, in Santa Rosa County, in 1914 is typical—even though we have no record of what brought these people together. Groups gathered, swapped information, gossip, and stories, and, after lunch, the younger people might choose up sides and play baseball. This custom would be eroded by World War I and devastated by World War II. In fact, countless little towns would disappear from the map—including Floridatown. (SPA)

AVIATION was to play as great a role in the modern development of Florida as the railroad, but who would have predicted this in 1911 when the box kite-like contraption, above, with James A. McCurdy at the controls, flew over Lake Worth, with the Royal Poinciana Hotel in the background? Miamians saw their first plane also in 1911 when the Wright aircraft, left, flown by Howard Gill, was demonstrated in celebration of the city's fifteenth anniversary. But aviation history was made in Florida in 1914 when pilot Tony Jannus began the first commercial air flights in the world, between St. Petersburg and Tampa. His flying boat *(below)* made two round trips daily for 187 days. First passenger was A. C. Pheil, who paid $400 for the honor of being the first passenger to fly on a regularly scheduled commercial airline. (SPA—Carson)

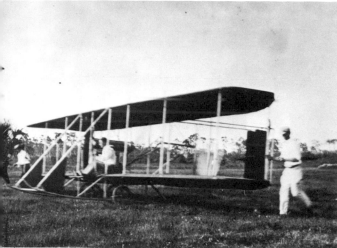

AVIATION had proved to be of small practical value until World War I when the belligerents sought to outdo each other in the development of aircraft causing the most destruction. A major step in the development of aviation in Florida occurred in 1914 when the Navy's first training station for aviators was established at the site of the abandoned Pensacola Navy Yard. The first class was called to duty in the middle of training to take part in the United States' occupation of Vera Cruz, with the result that both the first and second class were graduated in the same exercises in 1915. They are, seated, left to right: Richard C. Saufley, Patrick Bellinger, Kenneth Whiting, Henry Mustin. Albert C. Read, Earl Johnson, Alfred A. Cunningham, F. T. Evans, Edward G. Haas; standing, left to right, Robert R. Paunack, Earl M. Spencer, Jr., Owen Bartlett, Walter A. Edwards, Clarence K. Bronson, William M. Corry, Jr., Joseph P. Norfleet, Edward D. McDonnell, and Harold W. Scofield. Albert C. Read was to make the first airplane flight across the Atlantic, in 1919. Below is Lieutenant Commander W. M. Corry, Jr., of Quincy, first Floridian to enter Naval aviation. Corry Field at Pensacola is named for him. (U. S.—SPA)

159

FLIGHT TRAINING at Pensacola was related directly to naval tactics, and before the development of the aircraft carrier this meant operating flying boats, like those lined up on ramps at the Naval Air Station in 1914 *(above)*. Experimental work on the catapult developed rapidly, and in 1915 Lieutenant Commander Henry C. Mustin made the first catapult launching from a ship, off the stern of the *USS North Carolina* in Pensacola Bay. By 1917 the use of the catapult, like the Martin aircraft on the catapult of the *USS Huntington (left)* was part of aviation training. Lighter-than-Air also was a part of training. Below, a ground crew struggles to berth a DN 1 airship on a floating dirigible hangar at Pensacola in 1917. (SPA—U.S. Navy)

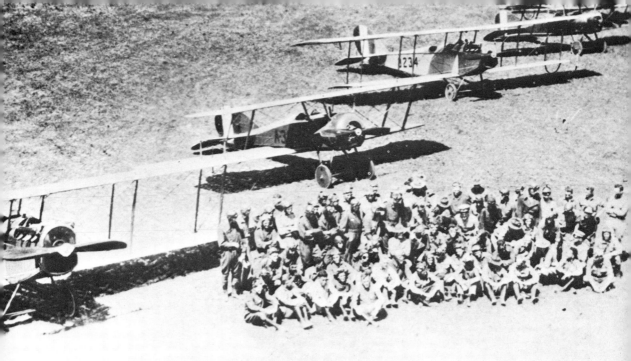

FLORIDA was selected for military flight training because of the large percentage of flying days during the year, and most airmen serving in World War I were trained here. The Navy established a training base at Miami's Dinner Key and greatly expanded training facilities at Pensacola, while the Marine Corps *(above)* selected a site in northwest Miami. The Army selected Arcadia, where major training and experimental facilities were established at Carlstrom Field *(below)*. A glance at the planes at Arcadia in 1918 tells you how far aviation had advanced in the four years since tests were made with the Wright experimental seaplane *(right)* at Pensacola Bay in 1914. Like many other planes built during that era, its principal value was in demonstrating what not to do in the design of an airplane. (SPA)

LET ME AT the Kaiser, the faces of these World War I draftees and volunteers seem to be saying as they line up in Tampa's Courthouse Square in preparation for departure to training camps. Floridians overwhelmingly supported the declaration of war against Germany and her allies, and citizens flocked to patriotic rallies, like the one below in Gainesville's Courthouse Square. (Dunn—SPA)

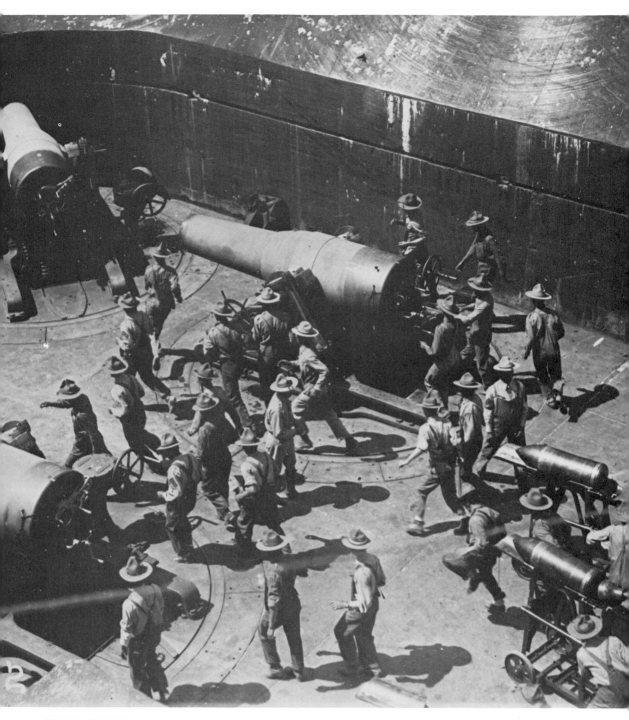

CUBAN CREWS man twelve-inch guns, set up in Fort Taylor to protect Key West during World War I. Although the guns were never fired in anger during the war, the crews went through daily drills in order to be alert and ready for action. Ironically, the guns were to fall into German hands during World War II. After Great Britain and France declared war on Germany in 1939, President Roosevelt ordered the guns sent to France where they were mounted on railway flatcars. The Germans outflanked the guns, presumably melted them down because they were obsolete, and fired the metal back at the Allies. (SPA)

QUIET RETURNED to Florida's rural communities after the end of World War I on November 11, 1918. This is Inverness on a sunny April 15, 1919, with an empty oak-shaded street leading to the courthouse, and three idle men sitting on the edge of a raised sidewalk whiling away the time. The rural communities had supported the war wholeheartedly, and early in 1919 entertained no doubts that the defeat of the Kaiser had been worth the sacrifices. But the revolutionary changes that began to take place in the 1920s caused many to wonder if they may not have won a war and lost the fruits of victory. (SPA)

*Opposite page:* THE PLACID SUWANNEE, made into a symbol of the romantic, care-free South by Stephen Foster, belies the tempestuous period that was about to explode in Florida after World War I. While Florida had been familiarly known to a generation of the rich leisure class, a war was needed to make it accessible to the average American. Moreover, developers and promoters succeeded in turning Florida into a make-believe tropical paradise which caught a nation's imagination and sparked one of the greatest real estate booms in history—the wild 1920s. (SPA)

# The Booming Twenties

GOD STILL LIVED in Heaven and William Jennings Bryan was a living Disciple when 5,000 met on Sundays in Miami's Royal Palm Park after World War I to hear the Great Commoner teach the "world's largest Bible class." Bryan, a frequent candidate for president, and, for a time, President Wilson's secretary of state, had a winter home in Miami. Although he had disagreed with Wilson over the conduct of foreign policies that were to get the United States involved in the war, Bryan was still one of the nation's most admired public figures. (SPA)

CRIME FLOURISHED after the war. An influx of new people contributed to it, but so did former servicemen who found readjustment to civilian life difficult, as well as those citizens who tried to circumvent the provisions of the National Prohibition Act. Law enforcement and legal institutions were put to a severe test. But decorum still reigned in court—as in this courtroom scene at Tampa. According to the calendar advertising "Sol Jacobs' General Insurance" behind the judge's bench, it is November, 1920. A jury is being sworn in for the trial of some unnamed miscreant who has run afoul of the law. Note the absence of women or blacks on the jury. Women had been given the right to vote when the states adopted the Nineteenth Amendment in August, 1920, but this applied to black women only in principle. By one means or another, usually through intimidation, blacks throughout the South were discouraged from voting. (Dunn)

SEA TURTLES came at night upon the beach at Key Biscayne in the early 1920s to lay their eggs—and men not only gathered the eggs but turned the turtles on their backs where they remained helpless until morning. Here the hapless turtles are being dragged to boats for a trip to some seafood restaurant. In time the turtles would stop coming. Taking both turtles and eggs reduced these great creatures to the verge of extinction. (SPA)

A NATION'S VIEW of what Florida was like before the estuaries and bays were despoiled by development was almost true. A tarpon, below, is brought to gaff in New River at Fort Lauderdale in the early 1920s. To catch a tarpon in New River in the 1970s would be as likely as a hunter bagging a dodo. Lake Worth, Biscayne Bay, and the Miami River were onetime fishermen's paradises, too. By the 1960s they had become so polluted that a fish needed greater protection than scales to survive. (Burghard)

167

PROSPERITY created by war, and travel made practical by the improvement of the motor vehicle, combined to put tens of thousands on roads leading to Florida. They were restless people. Many were looking for new opportunities, others were just looking, while a criminal element tagged along. They were, in a sense, like the Oakies who fled Oklahoma for California during the depression of the 1930s. Irritated Florida businessmen tagged them "tin can tourists," because they lived in tents, did their own cooking, and washed their own clothes. So many were the tin can tourists that communities, for sanitary reasons, were forced to establish camps, like the one at DeSoto Park, Tampa *(above)*, and at Gainesville *(below)*. Expanded police protection was required too. (SPA)

DESPITE ITS COST, World War I had created immense wealth, and many of more than moderate means flocked to Miami Beach where they could bask in ostentatious style at Carl Fisher's Flamingo Hotel. The occasion *(above)* is tea time in the Oriental Tea Garden. (Lest you forget, it was Prohibition time.) Most of the very rich and more sophisticated socialites preferred Palm Beach. The scene below is at The Breakers in 1926, newly opened after fire had destroyed the previous Breakers in March of 1925. Kermit Roosevelt, son of former President Theodore Roosevelt, wears a dark coat and white knickers. (SPA)

STYLES CHANGED rapidly in the post-war years, but it took the gals quite a while to get the bathing suit above their knees. The photograph *(above)*, made in the early 1920s, looks like it might have been more of a style-maker's effort than cheesecake. Most women above thirty were so modest that few of them would wear the new bathing suit styles. In the photograph *(below)* made at Roman Pools, Miami Beach, in 1923, hardly any women are seen in bathing suits. Most of them, wearing street clothes, are only watching. (SPA)

FESTIVE OCCASIONS, like the laying of the cornerstone for a new building at the University of Florida *(above),* brought the crowds out. And people could travel quite a distance now that everyone with a bit more than average earning power could own a car that cost $500 or under. The university was only fifteen years old at this time. (SPA)

THE STATE FAIR at Tampa *(below)* was well attended in the 1920s, and both adults and the kids had a great time. By the 1960s the nation's attitude would change so much that neither adults nor children could have cared less about fairs. Bah! They had seen it all—the amazing, stupendous, monstrous, horrendous, biggest, least, and the impossible. (SPA)

THE AUTOMOBILE virtually eliminated the horse after the war as a means of travel. Within the span of a single generation the car had changed the American way of life, even in a small town like Brooksville, in Hernando County *(above)*. Note the cleanliness of the paved street—so different from the days of the horse and the ever-present chirping sparrow. (SPA)

A CAMPER of 1922 vintage, forerunner of what was to come in the years ahead, parked in front of the Miami Chamber of Commerce *(left)*. We don't know where this couple came from, but a sign on the side of the box-like living quarters states: "We are going to the home of sunshine & palms, Miami, Fla." (SPA)

AN AMBULANCE operated by the King Undertaking Company, Miami, in 1922 *(below)*. With its high-pressure tires, it made a rough ride for the poor devil unfortunate enough to have to ride in it. But still it was a vast improvement over the days when the injured might be taken to the hospital in a wagon, bedded down in hay. (SPA)

KING COTTON lost its crown in the South after World War I. Invasion by the boll weevil was a major cause, but economic changes also contributed to cotton's downfall. This cotton-picking scene was in Leon County before the war. Florida at one time produced a sizeable amount of cotton, particularly Sea Island, a long-staple variety, which this field appears to be. The production of cotton in Florida was to cease altogether. (SPA)

TOMATO GROWING, unlike cotton, was affected little by the 1921 depression. Production methods, however, had not changed in twenty years, but yields were good in Dade County's marl soil. The field below was near Princeton. Planting was done in October and November, to catch the northern market when nobody else had tomatoes to sell. (SPA)

THE PLACID YEARS of the early 1920s would seem like a dream to Miamians after the strident years of boom and bust and the traumatic 1926 hurricane. A lone policeman stands at the intersection of East Flagler Street and Second Avenue on April 1, 1922, and you wonder where the traffic is that he's directing. Miami's water front in 1923 *(below)* was nothing like it would be in 1925, after most of the area in the foreground, and extending to the docks beyond the island in the middle distance, was filled for Bayfront Park and for the building of Biscayne Boulevard. From the number of cruising houseboats and yachts in port you know it is winter. Miami would never again enjoy the appeal it did the year this photograph was made—before the bayfront was filled, before the creation of the numerous islands in Biscayne Bay. (SPA)

THE LAND BOOM, which reached a crescendo in 1925, had its beginning in the prosperity and restlessness growing out of World War I, when millions of people began moving about the country in search of a new way of life. Thousands came to Florida—particularly to the Tampa-St. Petersburg-Clearwater and the West Palm Beach-Fort Lauderdale-Miami areas. Many bought property with the intention of building immediately, or later after they had saved sufficient money in those years before federal savings and loan associations. E. E. (Doc) Dammers *(above)*, ebullient auctioneer, sells lots in a subdivision near Miami in 1921. Dammers is standing in a wagon. (SPA)

AS THE BOOM approached its zenith George E. Merrick, builder of Coral Gables, employed the talents of silver-tongued William Jennings Bryan to sell lots. Bryan *(below)* is speaking from a platform set up in the Venetian Pool, Coral Gables. For his efforts, Bryan was paid $100,000 a year—half in cash, half in property. (SPA)

MIAMI WAS STILL an over-grown small town without a skyline in 1924, but in 1925 the steel work of a skyline began to rise, and within eighteen months it had been transformed into a city. Bayfront Park has been filled and planted *(above)* and major buildings are under construction along Biscayne Boulevard. By September 29, 1926, when the lower photograph was made, the transformation has been complete. The numbered hotels are the McAllister (only one built before the Boom), the Columbus, Colonial, and Everglades, in that order. The 1926 hurricane had hit eleven days earlier, which explains the absence of foliage. (SPA).

176

SPONTANEOUS though it appeared, many imaginative personalities were behind the Boom. One of them was wealthy Carl Fisher *(left,* in flop hat) who had helped John S. Collins and the Lummus brothers, J.E. and J.N., to develop Miami Beach. To sell the Beach and bring patrons to Fisher's hotels, he employed the talents of Steve Hannagan (bareheaded) who had put the Indianapolis Speedway on the map. But Florida was a magnet for promoters—like D.P. Davis of Tampa, Joseph W. Young of Hollywood, C. Perry Snell of St. Petersburg, Hugh Anderson of Miami Shores, James E. Bright and Glenn Curtiss of Hialeah, and George E. Merrick of Coral Gables. Most of them would go broke with the collapse of the Boom. Davis killed himself. (Miami Herald)

AN IRRESISTIBLE personality frequently identified with the spirit of the Boom was George E. Merrick, dreamer, poet, planner, builder, and seller of Coral Gables *(right).* Merrick looks directly at you while John McEntee Bowman, hotel chain owner and operator of the Miami Biltmore Hotel, studies the spokesman of the Boom admiringly. Bankrupt and penniless after the Boom, Merrick operated a fishing camp in the Florida Keys—property owned by his loyal wife, Eunice. (SPA)

NOTHING COMMONPLACE was allowed to distract from the planned beauty of Coral Gables. Even a water tank got full treatment. Construction *(left)* is begun to hide a water tower at Alhambra Circle and Greenway Court. When completed, the tank and its supporting structure are hidden behind a mock-up lighthouse *(right).* (SPA)

MIAMI BILTMORE HOTEL and Country Club was Merrick's outstanding construction achievement. Merrick lost the hotel to creditors after the Boom, and it was purchased by Henry L. Doherty, chairman of Cities Service. For a time in the 1930s it was in the wintertime a Florida extension of the White House during the New Deal Administration. Converted into a military hospital during World War II, it was to become a Veterans Administration hospital after the war. The city of Coral Gables became the owner after the VA moved out. (SPA)

AFFLUENCE AND WEALTH were attracted to Florida by the Boom. Cornelius Vanderbilt, Jr., and wife have just arrived in Miami by train. He founded the *Illustrated Daily Tab* in 1924, but closed it after the Boom. The Vanderbilts are in the stylish clothes of the period—she wearing mink and a hat that virtually covers her bobbed hair, while he carries a coon-skin coat on his arm and a walking cane in his hand. Bare headedness was rare, but you can bet he has his hat in his right hand, although it's not shown. (SPA)

BETTING ON HORSES was illegal, but when Hialeah opened in 1925 an overflow crowd of 17,000 jammed its clubhouse and grandstand. Miami's establishment financed and promoted the track, and Governor Martin in Tallahassee, responsible for seeing that Florida's laws were enforced, turned his head the other way. Hialeah attracted the socially elite and gave Miami class. Florida would get legal parimutuel betting in 1931. (Wright)

DRILLING FOR OIL at Oldsmar, in Pinellas County, brought out the curious *(above)* to see the hoped-for gusher, while *(below)* real estate boomers offer free barbecue to bring out the crowds. The "oil" well proved to be dry and the boomers went broke. To be identified with Tampa, the boomers changed the name of Oldsmar to Tampashores in 1925. By 1937 the townspeople would have enough of Tampashores, changing the name back to Oldsmar. (Dunn)

ILLEGAL PARKING became such a problem in Miami that police began collecting front seats from automobiles in the era before door locks became universal. The owner had to pay a fine to get back his seat. (SPA)

A MAJOR BOOMTIME project was the building of the new Dade County Courthouse. The lower portion was raised in 1925 about the old stone courthouse that had been built in 1904. After the lower part *(left)* was completed, the records were transferred from the old building to the new, and the old structure dismantled. Foundation for the new courthouse is being dug *(below)* by a power shovel. (SPA)

FLORIDA CITIES experienced their first traffic jams—automobile and pedestrian—during the Boom. Flagler Street *(above)* was a madhouse of activity. The parade of busses was common during the Boom when thousands of prospective buyers were brought to Miami free of charge to look at real estate and listen to the stirring sales talks of high-pressure salesmen. Tampa likewise had its cars and people. The scene below is at the Lafayette Street bridge over the Hillsborough River, with the Tampa Bay Hotel in the background. (SPA)

181

HIALEAH was the first city developed in what had been the Everglades before drainage. A twenty-foot tall Seminole Indian welcomed you to Hialeah in the 1920s. The bus-like vehicle is an Aero-Car, made in a local factory by Glenn Curtiss, aviation manufacturer and partner of James E. Bright in the development of Hialeah. (SPA)

DEVELOPMENT was intense through much of Florida during the Boom. New subdivisions appeared throughout countrysides, as though developers expected everybody in the United States to move to Florida. So many ships arrived at Miami with building supplies in 1925 that many had to anchor off the harbor entrance to wait their turn to get inside. Trucks of 1925 vintage *(below)* are being loaded at a Miami wharf. Note the solid rubber tires on the Mack truck in the foreground. (SPA)

THE HOTEL KELLEY of Gainesville, like many other Boom time structures, was abandoned after the "bust" without being completed. Acquired by the state, it was completed, renamed the Seagle Building, and turned over to the University of Florida. The building was for years the home of the Florida State Museum—until the 1970s when the museum got a new home on the university campus. (SPA)

UNABLE TO HANDLE all the Boom time traffic on a single track, officials of the Florida East Coast Railway decided in 1925 to double-track the line from Jacksonville to Miami. It proved to be very expensive, particularly because of the numerous new bridges that had to be built, including the one across the St. Johns River at Jacksonville. By the time the second track was ready for traffic, the Boom was over. (SPA)

WOMEN ENJOYED freedoms during the 1920s that had been denied their mothers. For instance, they could travel and work in cities away from home, which "decent" single women could not do before the war without suffering a stigma. But the pay for women was small and there were few places they could afford to stay. The YWCA sought to overcome this problem by providing cheap lodging. (SPA)

BOBBED HAIR was catching on throughout the nation in the middle 1920s, and gals in every kind of garb turned out for a "bobbed hair contest" at the Venetian Pool, Coral Gables. The first women to bob their hair at the end of World War I "shocked" the nation, but by 1925 the style was becoming accepted by all except the most conservative who thought the cutting of her hair was a disgrace to womanhood. (SPA)

THE FLAPPER AGE was exemplified by
Gilda Grey, entertainer, woman of the
world, and controversial image of female
sexual freedom. Miss Grey strikes a leggy
pose on a board walk at Miami Beach,
before the 1926 hurricane put an end to
board walks. (SPA)

185

FUN ON THE BEACH at Belleair included a portable record player and 78-
rpm records. And look how far bathing
suits have slipped above the knees in the
few years since the end of the war. (SPA)

WOMEN'S STYLES in 1924 de-emphasized the female shape, and, in general, were rather terrible, but must have been a major improvement in comfort over pre-war styles. While the younger women have their hair bobbed, none of the women of middle age or past do. Urchins wore their socks rolled below their knees, and shorts, like the one sitting on the step so proudly showing the camera a coconut. (Fisbaugh)

A FOURSOME at the Biltmore Country Club in 1924 includes hats for the women, knickers and jackets for the men. Knickers were popular for street wear, and they became the symbol of the "binder boys," those high-pressure salesmen who soared to the top during the wildest days of the Boom—and fell with an enormous thud when the Boom "went busted." (SPA)

"HELLO SUCKER," Texas Guinan seems to be saying to photographer G. W. Romer as she stands before the passenger train which brought her from New York to Miami for a night club engagement in 1925. It is a cold day and most of the men are wearing overcoats, but not Miss Guinan who knew that a gal, to shine, could not afford to hide her image and all those frills beneath a coat. (Romer)

186

MOST SPLENDID home built in Florida during the Boom was Ca'd'Zan, which John Ringling erected at Sarasota for his lovely wife, Mable. Modeled after the Doge's Palace in Venice, the mansion was her idea, and, to Ringling, nothing was too great or too expensive for his wife. But Mable Ringling was to enjoy her mansion only three years, dying in 1929 of Addison's disease at fifty-four. (SPA)

THE MASTER BEDROOM of the Ringling's included a barber's chair, which John Ringling found comfortable to rest his huge frame. In this chair he was not only daily shaved, but read the newspapers, kept up with the circus empire which he had helped to build, and made many important decisions. (SPA)

WHILE TRAVELING in Europe in search of circus talent, Ringling assembled a valuable collection of Renaissance and Baroque art, for which he had this museum built in the late 1920s. Ringling willed the museum and the grounds, including his mansion, to the state of Florida. The museum today houses what has been described as the finest collection of Baroque art in America, including four immense paintings by Peter Paul Rubens. A circus museum and the mansion also are open to the public. If you wish to enjoy full appreciation of Ringling's legacy, one of the finest to be found anywhere in the country, you need to know something of the circus king himself, whose life was the epitome of baroque. So go first to the circus museum, then to Ca'd'Zan, and last to the art museum. And take at least a day to see all. (SPA)

COLLECTED by Ringling on one of his several trips to Europe was this dwarf peasant carrying a market basket and smiling broadly. This is one of a dozen or so dwarf figures in a little garden at the rear of the Ringling Art Museum—a delightfully human thing that caught the circus king's eye.

KU KLUX KLANSMEN, dressed in their cleanest white, march into Miami's White Temple Methodist Church on a hot July day in 1926 to attend the funeral of a departed Klansman. Disturbing changes following World War I precipitated renewed interest in the Klan, and Klaverns were organized in the North as well as in the South, to "protect" communities from Reds, Bolsheviks, socialists, labor leaders, blacks, Jews, Catholics, foreigners, and foreign ideas. They worked with the police in many places, particularly in Miami, which explains why this street (Northeast Second Avenue) has been blocked off for the Klan. The KKK's misguided efforts eventually became obvious to its enlightened members, and in time the membership was reduced to a few hard core "rednecks." The downtown campus of Dade Community College occupies the site where White Temple stood in 1926. (Romer)

CALAMITY visited Miami on January 10, 1926, and stayed for a month—when the windjammer *Prinz Valdemar* sank in the channel leading to the Miami harbor. Meanwhile, a hundred ships, loaded with building materials, awaited unloading. Although the wildest part of the land speculation had passed, millions of dollars worth of construction, begun in 1925, was in progress, and many viewed this as evidence that the Boom would continue. But by the time the channel was cleared, much of the enthusiasm had vanished. It would take a major hurricane, however, to dispell the last hope of the more ardent boomers. (Hoit)

THE 1926 HURRICANE hit southeast Florida on the morning of September 18, taking more than 300 lives, injuring thousands, and leaving enormous property damage. The losses were due largely to poorly constructed buildings, like this concrete building, and to public ignorance about tropical storms. (SPA)

A COUPLE, Dr. Carl and Mrs. Scheffel, weathered the 1926 hurricane aboard this tough schooner, the *Kessie C. Price*. Unaware a hurricane was offshore, the Scheffels remained aboard on the evening of September 17 as the storm approached, and, as it moved across southeast Florida in the early hours of September 18, they could only hold on tight and hope for survival. The surging schooner was driven ashore, the anchor catching on the edge of a dock, and after the storm subsided and the tide dropped, the Scheffels found themselves "drydocked" in Bayfront Park. Dr. Scheffel was to practice medicine in Miami until his death in 1955. His widow, Belle, was living in 1974, remembering, at eight-six, the traumatic night of September 17-18, 1926, with a wry sense of humor. "It started with a gentle breeze out of the northeast," she said. (SPA)

190

DEMOLISHED, like the Hollywood Post Office *(above)* or badly damaged, like the Miami Beach home *(right)*, thousands of southeast Florida buildings showed a single major defect —they had not been designed and constructed to withstand hurricane winds. The result was a new building code, first adopted by Dade County, which required that beams and other important supports in block buildings be of poured concrete and contain a minimum amount of construction steel. The code also required that roofs be tied to beams. The home below is a classic example of a building whose construction violates just about every part of the hurricane building code now required in most Florida counties. (SPA)

DISASTER met the eye in every direction after the 1926 hurricane drove an eleven-foot tide over the Miami waterfront. Ships and barges and smaller craft were tossed ashore and left high and dry in Bayfront Park *(right)* and on Biscayne Boulevard.

THE MIAMI PLANT of the Florida Power & Light Company lost portions of its stacks in the 1926 hurricane. The roof is off the building at lower right, and the lumber yard, lower left, is a mess. (SPA)

192

BADLY DAMAGED by the 1926 hurricane, Miami's seventeen-story Meyer-Kiser Building had to be cut down to seven stories. The photograph at left shows the building as it was two weeks after the storm, with large areas of the walls missing and the structure in an obviously bent condition. The scaffolding was erected in preparation for dismantling and for the prevention of additional storm-damaged masonry falling into the street. Razing of the top ten stories is in progress at center, while at right is the sawed-off building as it looked several years later—as the American Bank Building. (SPA)

SOME OF FLORIDA was left after the hurricane, including the Coral Gables home that George E. Merrick had built of native limestone rock and masonry during the Boom. But, bankrupted by the "bust," Merrick soon would have to move out and turn his home over to creditors. (Fishbaugh)

THIS MAGNIFICENT locomotive, which the Florida East Coast Railway had acquired to cope with the mountainous freight and passenger traffic during the Boom, was big enough and heavy enough to survive any hurricane. But, alas, the company failed to survive. Heavily in debt in the face of declining revenues, the railroad had to throw in the sponge in 1931 and go into federal receivership. (SPA)

SPORTS GIANTS walked on earth just like other men in the 1920s, the era of "Babe" Ruth, Jack Dempsey, Gene Tunney, Lou Gehrig, and Bobby Jones—and they all made it to Florida. Dempsey *(below)* trains at Tampa in 1926, ostensibly for his upcoming match with Tunney, but the occasion was really a promotion of the new Forest Hills real estate development. Thousands turned out to see the famous world's champion prize fighter. (Dunn)

AMATEUR CHAMPION Bobby Jones prepares to putt one at the Miami Biltmore Country Club in 1928. He was national amateur champion in 1924, 1925, 1927, and 1928, and again in 1930. (SPA)

"BABE" RUTH, in knickers, comes out to watch the 1928 spring workout at St. Petersburg, but he isn't working today. In 1927 he had hit a record of sixty home runs, and he may have been holding out for more money. In uniform is Ruth's boss, Joe McCarthy, famed Yankee manager. (Dunn)

AUTOMOBILE RACES at the Tampa Fair in 1927 brought out an overflow crowd to see the little vehicles skid around the dirt track at fifty miles an hour, tossing up clouds of dust. (SPA)

A MAJOR FEAT of the era was the completion in 1928 of Tamiami Trail, which crossed Big Cypress Swamp and the Everglades between Naples and Miami. It had been a thirteen-year job—five years longer than was required to build the Overseas Railroad from the mainland to Key West. The digging was tough. Underneath the surface was hard limestone rock, requiring 40,000 pounds of dynamite per mile to pulverize it. A dynamite drill *(above)* is at work.

STRADDLING A CANAL, a dredge removes dynamite-pulverized limestone and piles it alongside to form the foundation for a highway. A road across southern Florida was suggested in 1914 by a Miami Herald reporter, William Stuart Hill, who promoted it through the mouth of James F. Jaudon, Dade County tax assessor. D. G. Gillette, secretary of the Tampa Chamber of Commerce, suggested the wedding of Miami and Tampa to get the name Tamiami Trail.

EARLY CONSTRUCTION of Tamiami Trail showed little to give hope that it would be completed. A. H. Andrews, who traveled what there was of the route in 1927, described it as "two ruts on a slight elevation." But the road was ready for traffic the following year, and the official opening was held in Miami on April 25, 1928. (SPA)

SELF-SERVICE GROCERY STORES made their appearance in the 1920s. This is a Handy-Andy Store in Miami in 1927. Another one was Piggly-Wiggly. Two additional self-service stores had the origin in the 1920s—Winn & Lovett in Jacksonville and Table Supply in Miami. They were later to combine, becoming Winn-Dixie. (SPA)

MAJOR AND SUBTLE changes were taking place in Florida in the late 1920s. The Port Everglades inlet was opened in 1928, permitting sea-going vessels into what was to become the largest port on the East Coast south of Jacksonville. It had been created by deepening and extending Lake Mabel, previously a four-foot deep body of water. In the distance is the New River inlet, later to be closed. (Hoit)

FLORIDA'S GREATEST disaster struck on the night of September 16, 1928, as a hurricane moving overland after thrashing the Palm Beaches, began to cross Lake Okeechobee. The furious wind carried a tide over the south shore, drowning 2,000 in one horrendous hour. The wreckage *(above)* is about the Pioneer Building in Belle Glade. The Belle Glade Garage was on the ground floor. Water and a 160-mile wind caused this damage. Pine coffins *(below)* arrive in the stricken area, but so many were the dead and so few were the coffins that hundreds of bodies—many unidentified—had to be piled up and burned. President Hoover initiated the building of a levee designed to protect lakeside residents from future hurricanes. (FCD)

FLORIDA'S FIRST Congresswoman, Ruth Bryan Owen, was elected in 1928. A resident of Miami, she was a daughter of the late William Jennings Bryan. Standing on the running board of her campaign car are her secretary and driver. Mrs. Owen was to be defeated in 1932 as she sought a third term. (Romer)

PRESIDENT-ELECT Herbert Hoover, visiting Miami on January 22, 1929, rides down Flagler Street in an open Lincoln as secret service men walk alongside or ride in following cars. Hoover had carried Florida over Catholic Alfred E. Smith by 144,168 to 101,764, the first Republican presidential victory in the state since 1876 when Republican Rutherford B. Hayes was selected over Democrat Samuel J. Tilden. Campaigners stumping the state for Hoover told Crackers that the pope was backing Smith, and declared that if elected Smith would receive his orders from Rome. (SPA)

WHAT THE CHIC GAL was wearing in 1929 is displayed here by Burdine's fashion models in Miami. In high-heeled shoes and with a generous show of legs, together with the demise of the flat-chested look, 1929 wasn't a bad style year. (SPA)

STYLES FOR SEMINOLE women in 1929 were on the conservative side compared with those for non-Indians. Beads, piled higher and higher about the neck, were a sign of affluence. This woman is wearing several pounds. The colorful skirt and blouse she probably made herself. Seminoles of both sexes wore their best clothes on ceremonial occasions and when on a visit to the city. (SPA)

FIRST MAN-MADE tourist attraction in Florida was the Singing Tower and Mountain Lake Sanctuary at Lake Wales, built by publisher Edward W. Bok as a monument to an idea—"to preach the gospel of beauty." The steel frame work *(above)* of the 205-foot carillon tower had its beginning in the spring of 1927. It is nearing completion at right, but the bells are yet to be installed. Workmen *(below)* guide the largest of seventy-one bells as a pulley begins the laborious task of raising the eleven-ton monster to the top of the tower. The smallest bell weighed eleven pounds.

200

REFLECTING ITS IMAGE in a quiet lake amid restful gardens, the Singing Tower drew 70,000 at its dedication on February 1, 1929, by President Calvin Coolidge. Below, Coolidge stands between Mrs. Coolidge, holding flowers, and Mrs. Edward Bok. Far right is Mr. Bok. Anton Brees, the late carillonneur who played daily concerts on the tower's bells, attracted thousands, and soon the Singing Tower was known throughout the United States. Much to the surprise of Bok, who had planned Mountain Lake Sanctuary as a quiet retreat for shy birds and introspective humans, the gardens atop 294-foot Iron Mountain quickly became one of Florida's leading attractions. Although still popular today, there is no admission charge; only a parking fee which is used to maintain a parking area and a paved road that winds through citrus groves to the sanctuary. (MLS)

MOONSHINING became a unique American industry in the 1920s after the adoption of the National Prohibition Act. The moonshine still *(left)* was found on the edge of the Everglades near Miami.

A MOCK-UP LOAD of lumber hid this cache of Canadian Club whiskey *(left)*, but "revenoo" officers spotted it and caught the unlucky driver. Much Canadian and Scotch whiskey was brought into Florida from the Bahamas by "rum-runners." So plentiful was good booze in Miami that it was little higher in price than moonshine. Below, a moonshine still is discovered in the deep woods of Hillsborough County by armed revenue officers. The barrels are for making corn mash, from which the white liquor was distilled. (SPA)

# The Depression Years

THE WORST DEPRESSION in America's history began on October 29, 1929, when the price bottom fell out of the stocks listed on the New York Stock Exchange. By the end of 1931 stock losses had reached an estimated $50 billion—about the equivalent of the Gross National Product for 1933—while unemployment was 15 million out of a total population of under 125 million. Florida was among the hardest hit states—but when you're out of work you might as well relax and enjoy baseball, as this crowd is doing in Jacksonville in front of the Florida Times-Union Building, where the progress of a world's series match between the St. Louis Cardinals and Philadelphia Athletics is being called out play-by-play. So many spectators have gathered in that pre-television era that the street intersection has been blocked. But that's all right. Few had money to buy gasoline to operate cars anyway. (SPA)

203

PANIC GRIPPED bank depositors as the 1930s began with the failure of bank after bank throughout Florida. The big boys who had promoted the Boom already had lost their money. Now it was the little man who was losing his, in busted banks. Moreover, there was no federal deposit insurance. The utterance of any rumor was enough to spark a run on a bank, and unless the bank had sufficient cash reserves it stood a good chance of running out of funds and being forced to close. This happened to the Central National Bank of St. Petersburg (above) on the morning of April 17, 1931, when anxious depositors began a run as the bank opened its doors at 9:00 a.m. According to the clock it is 10:05 a.m., and the bank has already shut its doors. Central National had been weakened by two previous runs and lacked the resources to survive this one. News of the bank's closing spread like wild fire, and within minutes a run was started on the Florida National Bank, above. This bank, with deposits of $1,761,995.95 and cash on hand of $152,146.12, would have been forced to close, but funds were rushed from sister banks in Lakeland, Bartow, and Jacksonville. Lines began to melt after depositors saw the green money stacked high about tellers' cages. Photographs of bank runs are rare. Newspaper files contain none, because publishers believed that the use of such pictures would trigger more runs. The shot of the crowd about Central National was made by John B. Green, while the shot below was made by a photographer at the orders of Edward Ball, then coordinator of Florida National Banks.

204

NOT ALL WAS GLOOM, despite bank runs and breadlines. Tampa's Miss Margaret Eckdahl *(right)* became "Miss America" in 1930. And Doc Webb's Poster Girls, below, demonstrating that where there is life there is hope, boosted the morale of St. Petersburg. Webb, owner of "The World's Most Unusual Drug Store," began the contest to publicize his business and St. Petersburg. (Dunn)

FLORIDA'S RICHEST resident in the 1930s was John D. Rockefeller, Sr., who maintained a winter home at The Casements, Ormond Beach *(left)*. Known to fellow residents as "Neighbor John," he was an ardent golfer who was frequently seen on the Ormond Hotel golf course, across the street from his home. Reaching ninety in 1929, Rockefeller had to cut his golf to six holes a day; but famous people came to play with him, including comedian Will Rogers. He traveled to and from Florida in his private railway car until 1937, when he died at Ormond Beach at the age of ninety-eight. He had been coming to Florida since shortly after his partner, Henry M. Flagler, acquired the Ormond Hotel in 1890. (SPA)

206

CATTLEMEN pooled horses, dogs, and manpower for cattle drives in the days of the open range, when Florida's tough cows roamed the countryside with more legal rights than a human. The cattlemen below prepare to drive Calvin Platt's cattle from Merritt Island to the mainland, over a bridge crossing Indian River and through the town of Cocoa. They are, left to right, Orvel Cox, Harney Partin, John Moyt, Marion Platt, Bud Yates, Bryant Cox, Reeves Hart, and John Partin. The herd stampeded through Cocoa, giving townspeople a fright they would never forget. In the foreground is a cattle dog, trained to herd cows. But in a stampede a dog could only flee for its life, because a herd would run right over it—or anything else.

MUCH OF FLORIDA was still frontier in the early 1930s, and land could be bought for one to five dollars an acre. Calvin Platt *(left)* of Melbourne owned over 100,000 acres in Brevard and Osceola counties and ran thousands of head of cattle on the open range. Although he could neither read nor write, he had no need to; he could keep everything in his head, and all he wanted in the way of a contract was a man's word. Platt carried as much as $10,000 in cash in his pocket, to pay his cowboys and to buy "a few more sections of land," or to buy a "good hoss" if he saw one. Although he failed to become a millionaire, some of his offspring would, as a result of the Space Age boom in Brevard County during the 1960s. (Platt)

OYSTER FISHING was engaged in by thousands, like the oysterman, right bringing up oysters with the aid of tongs from a bed in Apalachicola Bay. Although Florida's Gulf Coast was developed into one of the nation's major producers of oysters, the low prices forced a fisherman to work through the daylight hours six days a week to make a living. (SPA)

FLORIDA was still a rural state when the depression began, with a major percentage of its 1,468,000 population depending on farming, sawmilling, turpentining, or fishing to make a living. Cedar Key, below, was a poor fisherman's town during the depression, although a picturesque one. Its fishermen caught mullet for the "po' folks" and stone crabs for the tourists at Miami Beach. But the poor had no money, and Miami Beach restaurant owners, often broke themselves, had to ask for credit. (SPA)

COMMERCIAL AVIATION took a firm hold upon the air in the 1930s, and Florida played a major role in its development. America's first important international air lanes were opened from Miami to all parts of the world by Pan American Airways' Clipper flying boats, like those flying over Miami *(above)*. Below, the China Clipper, which flew between Miami's Dinner Key terminal and the Orient, has just arrived in port from China and Japan. The daily arrival of the Clippers was an event that drew hundreds of spectators who gathered to see the V.I.P.'s arriving—Charles A. Lindbergh, Will Rogers, General Douglas MacArthur, Lionel Barrymore, and high-ranking United States and foreign government officials. Pan American had its origin at Key West in 1927, with the inauguration of flights between Florida and Cuba. (SPA—Pan Am)

EASTERN AIRLINES began the first regular passenger service between Miami and New York on January 1, 1931, with six-passenger Kingbirds, above. In 1934 Captain Eddie Rickenbacker's airline inaugurated dawn-to-dusk flights between Miami and New York, using the sleek DC-2. (Eastern)

NATIONAL AIRLINES was born in St. Petersburg in 1934, with the mail contract to Daytona Beach by way of Tampa, Lakeland, and Orlando. Ted Baker's line soon added Stinsons, carrying passengers as well as mail. Baker, below, in shirt sleeves, poses with passengers in front of a 1935 vintage Stinson.

THE MIAMI All-American Air Maneuvers drew thousands of aviation enthusiasts in the 1930s—and the military joined in, too, in order to display their aircraft and the skill of their pilots. Above is a race, with planes making turns about a pylon. The nation's outstanding pilots could be seen here, but the air meets were dangerous and a number of pilots lost their lives.

THE AUTOGYRO, forerunner of the helicopter, did prove to have a future. Although a conventional type plane with a rotor on top, it required only a little space for landing or take-off, as was proved by the pilot who brought his autogyro down in Bayfront Park in Miami. (SPA)

THE DIRIGIBLE *Akron* visited Florida in January, 1933, and moored at Opa-Locka. For a time it appeared that the huge airships might be the coming way of travel, and, because of their ability to fly long distances, the military was testing their possible use in war. The burning of the zeppelin *Hindenburg* in 1937 at Lakehurst, N.J., with a loss of thirty-six lives, put an end to talk about the future of dirigibles. (SPA)

TRAVEL BY TRAIN was by far the most popular way of travel in the 1930s, although travel by bus was growing. Only a few of the more sophisticated flew, while a lack of a paved highway system and the uncertain performance of the motor car made driving long distances risky and a chore. At the end of Miami's winter season as many as five sections of the Florida East Coast Railway's Florida Special were needed to carry all those returning north. Five locomotives with steam up *(above)*, await orders to pull out one at a time. In the background is the Dade County Courthouse. The Jacksonville Terminal *(below)*, one of the busiest in the South, was Jacksonville's outstanding building in the 1930s. (Hoit—JHS)

211

A TRAUMATIC NIGHT for Miami occurred on February 15, 1933, when Guiseppe Zangara, a mad unemployed bricklayer, made an attempt on the life of President-elect Franklin D. Roosevelt in Bayfront Park. Although Zangara fired five bullets and hit five people, he missed Roosevelt. Among those hit was Mayor Anton Cermak of Chicago, standing beside the open car in which Roosevelt *(left)* was sitting. Cermak *(right)* has just received the fatal bullet. He was to die in Jackson Memorial Hospital of peritonitis on March 6. On March 20, fourteen days after Cermak's death, Zangara sat in the electric chair at Raiford Prison, and, when asked by Sheriff Dan Hardie of Dade County if he had anything to say, replied "Pusha da button."

BAYFRONT PARK Bandshell, with the Miami skyline in the background, was the scene of the assassination attempt. The president-elect, accompanied by Miami Mayor R. B. Gautier in the rear seat of a convertible, made a short talk from the vehicle as it was parked among the royal palms near the bandshell. He had just finished greeting Mayor Cermak, an old political friend, when Zangara *(below)* began firing. (Miami Herald)

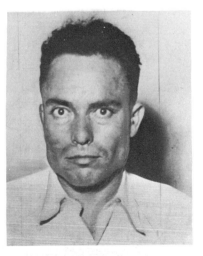

213

LAST GREAT STANDS of Florida's virgin cypress timber were cut in the 1930s and 1940s, except for some in Big Cypress Swamp, which went to the mill in the early 1950s. A Crummer Cypress Company train *(left)*, hauls big logs to the firm's sawmill at Lacoochee *(below)*. Note the enormous yard of lumber stacked for seasoning. (SPA)

CYPRESS TREES were "deadened" *(left)* six to twelve months before cutting, to make the trees "shed" their water and thereby lightening them by more than one-half their original weight. Deadening was required to make the trees float, if they were to be rafted downstream to a mill.

MILLWORK in Crummer and other lumber company plants *(below)* gave work to thousands of Floridians, but the work ended after the last trees were cut, and the mills shut down. (SPA)

214

SAWMILL TOWNS in uncounted numbers were abandoned in the 1920s, 1930s, and 1940s after the last major stands of virgin timber was cut. Here is a nameless village, the shacks and outhouses decaying and falling apart, and with the dogfennel and grasses growing where children once played. Eventually such towns disappeared completely, rotting or burning in woods fires. Bricks were salvaged and carried away, and in time every sign of human habitation vanished, except the cemeteries. The cemetery *(right)* is all that remains to show that the community of Varnom once existed near Panama City. Some of the headstones are recent, indicating that at least a few of those who abandoned the community eventually returned to join their forebearers and stay indefinitely. (SPA)

AN ARTIST'S DELIGHT, perhaps, and certainly a quail hunter's dream, this rural scene was a familiar one in the 1930s in north Florida, but its day was passing. This cabin—it once could have been quarters for a black or white sharecropper family—stands empty and is decaying. A woods fire probably would be the end of it, saving its owner the trouble of dismantling an old building. Fields and woodlands like these are where you find covies of plump quail when the hunting season opens in the fall. But the freshness of the plowing tells us it is perhaps February and the farmer has turned the land in preparation for spring planting. The quail covies that survived the hunting season are still together, but the cocks are sidling up to the hens and beginning to challenge each other as the mating season approaches.

PULP AND PAPER mills, requiring thousands of cords of pine wood daily, followed the sawmills in the 1930s after the big pine timber had been cut. These mills could use second-growth trees too small for timber. After the bark is removed, the wood is sliced into chips which are reduced to pulp, most of which goes into kraft paper, used either for bags or wrapping paper, or for the manufacture of corrugated boxes. Enormous pulpwood requirements for such mills as the St. Joe Paper Company at Port St. Joe *(above)* and the Rayonier Pulp and Paper Manufacturers at Fernandina *(below)* made it necessary for the development of a major reforestation program in Florida. By 1970 Florida would have nine pulp and paper mills. Meanwhile, state and private plant nurseries were producing some 200 million pine seedlings a year for reforestation. (SJPC—SPA)

216

CIGAR-MAKING machines in the 1930s were taking over a job formerly done by deft fingers. At one time 13,000 were employed in the hand-rolling of cigars, as in the Tampa plant *(above)* at an earlier era. Looking closely, you can spot the "reader," on an elevated platform near the upper right corner. His job was to read newspapers and magazines to entertain the workers in the days before piped-in music. A few modern machines operated by women *(right)* turn out more cigars in a day than hundreds of men using the old method. (SPA)

MECHANIZATION did not lend itself to all jobs, like strawberry packaging or canning at Plant City *(below)*, which required individual handling of the berries. Plant City was for a time one of the nation's largest producers of strawberries. (SPA)

SEX began shedding centuries of taboos in the 1930s as specialists offered advice to the married. But there was still enough embarrassment that the "professors of sex" talked to husbands and wives separately, as the huge sign on a Tampa streetcar reveals. (SPA)

SIGNS OF THE TIMES flash out at you from these Depression-times scenes. A six-room house and three-room cottage on a 50 by 150 foot lot in Fort Lauderdale are offered for $2,500.00. At the cigar and soda stand *(below)* in Miami, milk shakes are ten cents and cigarettes fifteen cents. The highest-priced sandwich, baked ham, is fifteen cents. (Burghard—SPA)

TO CREATE jobs for artists during the Depression, the WPA established projects like these for the decoration of federal buildings, many of which were constructed during that period. The mural *(above)* entitled *Discovery*, depicting the landing of Ponce de Leon in Florida, was done by Charles Hardman for the Miami Beach Post Office, while the mural *(below)* entitled *Osceola Holding Informal Council with His Chiefs*, was done by Lucille Blanch for the Fort Pierce Post Office. (SPA)

UNFORGETTABLE is the only way to describe a Sunday excursion from Miami to Key West in the early 1930s on the "train that went to sea." The round-trip ticket was about $2.50. You returned the same day—but what an interesting day it was. Crossing the long bridges *(above)* you felt you were at sea. But the railroad was abondoned after the fierce Labor Day Hurricane hit on September 2, 1935, leaving 500 dead and twenty miles of destruction to road bed and bridges. (Perez)

THE OVERSEAS HIGHWAY to Key West, built on the roadbed and bridges of the abandoned railroad, was opened in 1938. The old Bahia Honda railroad bridge served as the roadbed for an automobile highway, built atop the steel trusses supporting the wide spans over the deep Bahia Honda channel. (SPA)

CORAL GABLES was sparsely settled in 1935 when photographer G. W. Romer made this aerial shot of "Cardboard University," first home of the University of Miami, at University Drive and University Court. The exterior walls were but a facade, the interior being of the cheapest kind of construction. Students often found themselves listening to the instructor in the next room. After the university moved to its present campus following World War II, this building was razed. (SPA)

CONCERN for the welfare of migrant agricultural workers had its beginning in the 1930s when living conditions like these were publicized by the press. The car bears a 1936 Tennessee license, but the scene is at Winter Haven.

MIGRATORY WORKERS paid $2 a week for these cabins at Belle Glade in 1939.

THIS EMERGENCY camp was set up at Pahokee to provide simple shelter.

A JUKE JOINT at Moore Haven, where a fellow could take his girl, buy a Coke to chase down cheap liquor, and do a little hand-holding and necking while a juke box blared out the "country" hits of the era.

"WHITE & COLORED" were served at the Choke 'Em Down Lunch Room at Belle Glade *(below)* two decades before Florida integrated its public eating places. But this lunch room was patronized mainly by black and white migrants who were accustomed to working together in the bean fields of the rich Everglades.

A BLACKJACK game is in progress at Moore Haven, with the dealer collecting the silver of a bettor who has called for a card that "busted" him, resulting in his automatically losing the hand. The players are making the dealer, or banker, deal out of the box the cards came in, so he can't "spook up" a card from the center of the deck. (SPA)

SOME HAD MONEY to play the horses even in the middle 1930s—and they poured into Miami during the winter to attend the races at beautiful Hialeah Park. Revenue received from parimutuel betting was of immense help during the Depression to Florida counties, who shared in it equally.

BUILDER of Hialeah Park, wealthy Joseph E. Widener of Philadelphia, proved that you could overcome the Christian conscience of Florida's "bible belt" counties by offering them equal shares in the distribution of parimutuel betting revenues. Opposition to the legalizing of betting ceased, and the 1931 Florida Legislature passed the bill over the veto of the moralistic governor, Doyle Carlton, Sr. (Miami Herald)

MIAMI BEACH was the first city in Florida to recover from the Depression, because of its "discovery" as an ideal winter vacationland by those who had money to blow. The Beach's population quadrupled in the 1930s, growing from 6,494 in 1930 to 28,000 in 1940. By the end of the decade 75,000 visitors were coming down each winter to occupy the increasing numbers of hotels. In the above photograph, made in 1940, hotel row has begun to extend well north of the Roney Plaza Hotel the large towered building on the oceanfront. (MBPD)

224

PUBLICITY AND PROMOTION brought the people of Florida—and nobody new it better than Everest G. Sewell (below, left), who helped to found Miami in 1896. Sewell organized the Miami Chamber of Commerce and served for years as its secretary, even during the several terms he served on the Miami City Commission or as mayor of Miami. Here he is in the office of the Miami Publicity Bureau, talking with Director Hamilton Wright, Jr., in the 1930s. Sewell, incidentally, was mayor at this time. But people called him Mayor Sewell, whether he was in office or out. (SPA)

FATHER JEROME, mite-sized Benedictine priest but of enormous size spiritually, became widely know in the 1920s and 1930s during his travels in sparsely-settled Florida. The 95-pound, pixie-like monk arrived at Saint Leo Abbey in 1908 and was to remain there for the rest of his life as a worker in the groves and gardens, as well as a teacher and itinerant priest. Walking and hitchhiking, he traveled over much of the peninsula, saying mass when other priests were unavailable, and visiting Catholic families living in isolated areas. Widely known among non-Catholics, he was fed and bedded by Baptists, Methodists, and Presbyterians as well as by Catholics—for wherever night caught him he was welcome. He was to live until 1966, dying at 81.

RISING from a tropical setting of palms and surrounded by orange groves, Saint Leo Abbey stands atop a hill from which it commands a magnificent view of the countryside in Pasco County. Benedictine monks, who established the abbey in 1889, for a time raised their food, including beef, pork, and poultry, but, after demonstrating that good grapes could not be grown in Florida, turned to citrus for cash income. Their groves helped to expand the abbey, where in the early part of this century some twenty-five priests, thirty brothers, and a dozen or so students studying for the priesthood lived. A summer camp for boys expanded into a public school, and, in the 1960s, into Saint Leo College, a four-year institution attended by both sexes. A modern college campus has been added since the era depicted here. (SPA)

MANY FAMOUS WRITERS have had homes in Key West, and most of them used the area as settings for novels, plays, or short stories. Best known was Ernest Hemingway *(left)* who lived at the home *(below)* on Whitehead Street in the 1930s. Hemingway's novel, *To Have and Have Not,* used Key West as a setting. And Hemingway wrote at least a part of his famous Spanish Civil War novel, *For Whom the Bell Tolls,* at Key West. Maxwell Anderson used the keys as a setting for a one-act play, *Key Largo,* while Thelma Strabel's novel, *Read the Wild Wind,* is about Key West. Many artists have been attracted to Key West, too, including John James Audubon, in 1832, and Winslow Homer, who visited Key West several times between 1888 and 1903. The Hemingway home is now operated as a museum.

THE POLITICAL TREND was reflected in the overwhelming vote received in the 1938 primaries by U.S. Senator Claude Pepper against powerful opponents—242,350 against 110,675 for Congressman J. Mark Wilcox and 52,417 for former Governor Dave Sholtz. Winning the Democratic primaries was tantamount to winning the election. Pepper was to carry Florida easily against all opponents until 1950 when the changing political tide swept conservative George Smathers into office. Because of his support of Roosevelt's New Deal, Pepper was a national figure in 1938, and reporters were sent from newspapers out of state to cover the campaign—like this unidentified newsman sitting on the running board of a Claude Pepper campaign car to peck out his story from "on the road." (SPA)

227

SUBSISTENCE farming, when a rural family produced virtually all of its food, was rapidly coming to an end with the approach of the 1940s. But a few hold-overs of a long-time way of life remained for a time—such as cane grinding and syrup making, and the grist mill, like this one in Escambia County, where you could take a sack of shelled corn and have it ground into grits or meal. The quality of the supermarket product might have been inferior, but it would win out. It cost too much to grow your own corn and it took too much time to shell the corn and take it to mill. Life really had changed. (SPA)

"EVERY BUILDING is out of the ground, into the light . . . a child of the sun . . . the first truly American campus," is the way Frank Lloyd Wright described the buildings he designed in the 1930s for Florida Southern College at Lakeland. Much of the early construction was done by students, under the direction of Wright's resident assistant, Nils Schweizer, because the college lacked funds to employ professional builders. Annie Pfeiffer Chapel *(above)* was the first and is the best known of the seven Wright buildings on the campus—largest collection of Wright's architecture in a single location in the world. Although completed in the early 1940s, the building looks more like one which might have been constructed in the 1960s or 1970s, demonstrating Wright's influence on architecture.

228

ALTHOUGH BROKE and without foreseeable funds to pay anyone so high-priced as Frank Lloyd Wright *(right)*, FSC President Ludd M. Spivey induced the architect to design the buildings on the promise he would "work day and night" to raise funds to pay for them. Wright is shown at one of his inspection visits during construction. He praised the students' work. (Florida Southern College)

ARCHITECT Nils Schweizer checks a blueprint with a student during construction of the Frank Lloyd Wright complex of buildings at Florida Southern College. Following directions by Schweizer and Wright, who designed forms for the making of unique building blocks and other building parts, students with no previous construction experience proved they could do work equal to that of professionals.

AMONG THE UNIQUE writers in Florida's history, Marjorie Kinnan Rawlings, settled with her husband, Charles, at Cross Creek in Alachua County in the late 1920s. Charles gave up the struggle of trying to earn a living from writing in the back country of Florida, but Marjorie struggled through the Depression, and in 1939 won a Pulitzer Prize for her novel, *The Yearling*. Then, in 1942, her *Cross Creek*, a book about the residents of her community, was published. It hit like a bomb. A few of the people who came out somewhat earthy, and without the author bothering to change their names, were embarrassed—and one, Zelma Cason, sued. But *Cross Creek* became part of American literature and her characters would enjoy an immortality denied most. The Cracker type home *(left)* where Mrs. Rawlings lived until her death in 1953 has been restored and is operated as a museum by the state.

THIS OLD BARN, which served a useful purpose during the residence of Marjorie Kinnan Rawlings at Cross Creek, has been dismantled. In addition to her writing, Mrs. Rawlings raised citrus, and Snow Slater, a character in *Cross Creek*, was her grove manager. The author gave Slater and his wife a twelve-acre home site on Orange Lake.

GEORGE FAIRBANKS *(left)*, a never-do-well with a cleft palate, proposed to Mrs. Rawlings after his house burned down. He's dead and gone from natural life, but, as a character he will live on in *Cross Creek* as the preposterous lover.

WILL MICKENS *(right)* also is a character in *Cross Creek*—but Mrs. Rawlings was less kind to him than to his wife, Old Martha, her cook. Mickens was to live to be ninety-nine, dying at Hawthorne in 1966. He was pleased to have been mentioned in the book.

IN PRE-WAR YEARS citizens could spend a quiet afternoon in a city park, like Mirror Lake in St. Petersburg, without fear of being mugged. But no era is closed to the bizarre, like the discovery in Key West in 1940 that Karl von Cosel had been living with the corpse of a beautiful young woman, Elena Hoyos Mesa, with whom he had fallen in love before her death seven years earlier. Von Cosel, the goateed man being questioned *(below),* said he was working on a "formula" to restore the girl's life, and he petitioned the court to let him keep the body in his possession. This was denied, but the perverse old man escaped prosecution. He subsequently died at Zephyrhills, Florida, protesting to the end his love of the corpse. (Dunn—W&L)

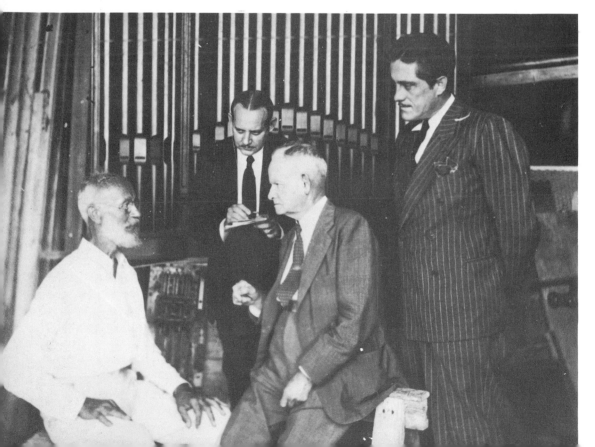

# Florida since 1940

FOREVER IDENTIFIED with elderly people, St. Petersburg's famous sidewalk benches on a carefree pre-war day draw the young as well as the aged. World War II would end the carefree days and bring Florida's tourist economy to a standstill. But the military installations that were to accompany the war effort would more than make up for the loss. (Dunn)

TENS OF THOUSANDS of young men from all over the nation saw Florida during World War II when they were sent here for training in preparation for joining combat forces overseas. In this scene at Miami Beach, men line up as far as you can see for their morning exercises before attending classes in the ocean-front hotels, taken over by the military for classrooms and dormitories. These are future Army Air Corps (now Air Force) officers for the mighty bomber fleets and fighter squadrons with which the United States was to pound Germany and Japan. Preparing for the possible use of poison gas by the enemy, these men exercise while wearing gas masks. Florida was to see many of these men again after the war, when they returned to make their homes, igniting a growth boom that would virtually quadruple the state's population in thirty years. (SPA)

THE WAR EFFORT drew every able-bodied man, either into the military service, production, or construction. The men at left are lined up before a Florida State Employment Service office at Camp Blanding, in preparation for signing up as construction workers on that huge military base near Starke. Below, the building of a barracks is in progress. At the height of wartime training, the Army had as many as 30,000 at Camp Blanding at one time. Most Florida men entering the military services were processed here. (SPA)

IN ITS BATTLE against Nazi submarines prowling the waters about Florida, the Caribbean, and the Gulf of Mexico during the war, the Navy used blimps for reconnaissance. Richmond Field, twenty miles southwest of Miami, was selected as the main base, and here three huge hangars, each larger than a football field and the equivalent in height of a sixteen-story building, were built. Until destroyed by fire during the 1945 Hurricane, they had the reputation of being the largest wooden structures in the world. (U.S. Navy)

THOUSANDS of aviation students learned to fly at Pensacola during World War II in the Navy's famous SNJ, a noisy but dependable airplane. After graduation, students went on to advanced training in fighter or bomber planes at other bases. But it was at the Pensacola Naval Air Station that they earned their wings in a course that was a mental as well as physical grind. (U.S. Navy)

BLIMPS, used by the Navy in its war against submarines, swing about their moorings at Key West while crews take a respite from long hours of duty at sea. (W&L)

234

GUYS AND GALS find time for fun during periods between studies and training at Miami Beach. Left to right, are Private Clarence Muller, Toni Sorrell, Helene Huntress, and Private Perrin Sample. (Miami Herald)

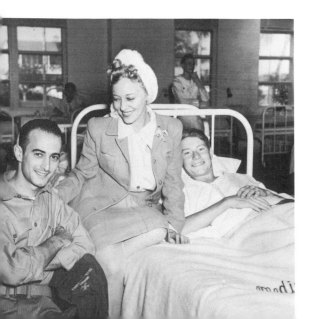

FAN DANCER Sally Rand, a Key West winter resident, cheered patients during her frequent visits to the Naval Hospital during the war.

A TWELVE-INCH GUN is test-fired at Fort Pickens during war. It was part of a battery set up to protect the Pensacola Naval Air Station and Pensacola from enemy ships approaching from the Gulf. (SPA)

DEMONSTRATING their devotion to flag and country during World War II, the staff and students of Florida State College for Women make a "V" for Victory on the campus at Tallahassee. The time is 1942, a dark year in U.S. history. The Japanese not only had destroyed our Pacific fleet at Pearl Harbor, but had seized our military bases in the Far East, while German submarines were sinking our freighters and tankers within sight of the Florida coast. Such demonstrations as this were common at a time when the nation not only was fighting for its existence, but when many had sleepless nights worrying about the outcome. (SPA)

HURRICANES gave Florida a wide berth during World War II, but immediately thereafter resumed the fury the state had known periodically as far back as the history of the peninsula is recorded. A hurricane on September 15, 1945, hit south Dade County with 150-mile winds, doing extensive damage. But the most spectacular side effect was a fire of mysterious origin during the height of the storm, which destroyed the Navy's three huge hangars at Richmond Field. When it was over nothing was left of the hangars but the massive end doors and charred wreckage. (Miami Herald)

237

STORMS wrecked homes along the Atlantic coast during the late 1940s and in the 1950s, by incessantly pounding the shore until foundations were undermined and the building fell onto the beach. How to save Florida's shore line became a major problem. (USCE)

*Opposite page:* VICTORY did come, following nearly four years of costly war, and among the happy ones were the servicemen—like those aboard the USS submarine Seadragon, in port at Key West on V-J Day after a long campaign against Japanese ships in the Far East. (W&L)

DISTINGUISHED black educator, Mary McLeod Bethune, founded her own school—now Bethune-Cookman College—at Daytona Beach in 1904, with $1.50 in capital. Although her capital was to grow very little during the next twenty years, Dr. Bethune herself became widely known and respected. During the Roosevelt administration she was an adviser to the President on black education. Here she is in 1943, at age sixty-eight, saying goodbye to students upon retiring. She was to see her school become a nationally respected institution before her death in 1955. (SPA)

DURING AND AFTER the war President Harry Truman was a frequent visitor to Key West, staying at the "Little White House," in a tropical setting on the Naval Station. Here the Navy turns out to honor him during an inspection tour. The civilian in background is John M. Spottswood of Key West, close friend of the President. (W&L)

PRESIDENT TRUMAN dedicated the Everglades National Park at Everglades on December 6, 1947. (Miami Herald)

EVERGLADES NATIONAL PARK, a wilderness consisting of saw grass, tree islands, mangrove forests, shallow bays and estuaries, was worthy of preservation not only because of its own distinctive character, as above, but also because of its fantastic numbers of wildlife, like the ibis, herons, and other aquatic birds taking flight, below. It covers 1,400,000 acres in southern Florida. (SPA—Miami Herald)

239

A MORALITY campaign, begun during the war, continued in Miami after the servicemen had gone home, as lawmen and newspapers campaigned against casino gambling, horse bookmaking, prostitution, and strip-tease shows. Captain H. S. Redmon, left, and Police Chief H. Leslie break up gambling equipment seized in a raid. (Miami Herald)

A BIT OF STRIP-TEASE is demonstrated in the Dade County Courthouse elevator (above) by members of a Jungle Club show, arrested for allegedly showing too much body. They are on their way to the county jail, to be booked on charges of being "lewd, lascivious," and whatever else arresting officers can find in the statutes to throw at them.

MANY CHANGES occurred in Florida as a result of World War II, but life among the Seminoles remained much the same as it had been at the turn of the century. Most of the Indians lived in chickees, on the edge of canals or sloughs in the wilderness, as the one at left. Many were beginning to drive the white man's car in preference to traveling in dugout canoes. (SPA)

DEACONESS Harriet Bedell, Episcopal missionary, enjoyed a warm relationship with the Seminoles, many of whom treated her like one of the family. Although she failed to win many souls, she convinced the Indians that whites could be good people when they tried. Her failure to stop the exhibition of Indians by whites as tourist attractions bothered her almost as much as her failure to Christianize them. Here she is with the family of Ingraham Billie, a Seminole medicine man. This is typical of the way Seminoles lived in 1950, sitting about a fire while the mother cooked in a cast iron pot. (SPA)

FLORIDA AGRICULTURE, which had suffered during the Depression as subsistence farming disappeared, became a major source of the state's income after the war, second only to tourism. Greatest developments were in winter vegetable production and citrus. The spraying machine *(above)* sprays twelve rows of sweet corn at a time, on a farm in the rich muck soil near Lake Okeechobee. (Miami Herald)

241

TWO HARVESTING RIGS *(below)*, each with a crew of seventy-five cutters, packers, and handlers, harvest fifty-four rows of celery at a time near Belle Glade. The celery is packed into crates on the machine, loaded into trucks, and hauled to a plant where it is rapidly cooled for shipment to northern markets the same day. (Miami Herald)

HAND-PICKING was the only way to get citrus off the trees, and still would be in the mid-1970s, although scientists were close to the perfection of a mechanical picker. (SPA)

POPULARITY of frozen citrus concentrate, perfected during the war, created such a demand for oranges that thousands of new groves were planted, making Florida the world's major citrus producing area. The rolling citrus country *(below)* is south of Leesburg. (SPA)

CUTTIN' SUGARCANE is the "hardest work in the world," and few will do it if they can find any other way to make a living. Most sugarcane was harvested by Jamaicans, adept in wielding machetes, until the 1970s when some growers began using a mechanical harvester developed in Australia. (SPA)

POTATO HARVEST was mostly hand-work, except for the "digging" *(left)*, which was done by a machine. Dade County's red-skinned potatoes, harvested in February, were the earliest potatoes produced in the United States. And potatoes were still being grown in Dade in 1974, but real estate developments were threatening.

PICKING UP and putting potatoes into field crates *(above)*, and grading potatoes *(left)* after they are washed and waxed at the Frederick C. Peters Farms, south Dade. Deformed and injured tubers are removed. (Burghard)

LOADIN' watermelons can be fun, because there's always the sure chance of one being dropped—and nothing's better than the heart of a "busted" watermelon.

THE UNIVERSITY OF FLORIDA, prior to World War II, was principally an agricultural, engineering, and law school. And while the university was to grow enormously in all branches of education after the war, its agricultural research department was quietly revolutionizing the production of citrus, cattle, and winter vegetables. Greatest improvements were made in nutrition, for both animals and plants, while a better selection of animal breeds and plant varieties, together with control of insects and diseases, put new wealth in farmers' pockets. The University was having growing pains in 1947, when this aerial shot was made, and numerous temporary buildings were erected to handle the overflow of students. (SPA)

INTRODUCTION of Brahman cattle, which were crossed with English breeds, gave Florida's cattle industry its greatest boost. Here is part of the Brahman herd owned by Henry O. Partin of Kissimmee, in 1952, including "Old Emperor," twelve-year-old champion bull. (SPA)

LAWRENCE SILAS, black cattleman of Kissimmee, won wide acclaim for his knowledge of cattle in the era of the open range. Silas was one of the few blacks who ran a herd of his own, competing with white cattlemen for grass. A story about Silas, written by Zora Neale Hurston, Florida's best known black writer, appeared in the September 5, 1942, issue of *Saturday Evening Post*. (Miami Herald)

THE COW CREEK branch of the Seminole Indians ran cattle in north Florida while the peninsula was Spanish owned, but were forced to abandon their animals during the wars with the United States. Then, in the 1930s, during the Midwest "dust bowl," hundreds of starving cattle were shipped from grassless ranges to Florida and sold to the Seminoles at nominal prices. With the help of experts, the Indians improved pastures; the cattle grew fat and herds increased. Seminoles (below) brand a yearling during a roundup at the Brighton Seminole Indian Reservation, northwest of Lake Okeechobee. (SPA)

FLORIDA CATTLEMEN were so powerful politically that for years they were able to prevent the passage of a state law requiring the fencing of pastures. The result was that cattle roamed the highways with more rights than a human driving an automobile—like the animals *(above)* on what is today John F. Kennedy Boulevard in Tampa. One editor, campaigning in his newspaper against the "open range," suggested that highways be renamed "bullevards." Fuller Warren, a native of Blountstown, in northwest Florida, ran for governor in 1948 on a promise to force the cows off the highways. Elected, he accomplished it, although with heated objection from the more conservative cattlemen. Campaigner Warren *(below)* shakes hands with Lake Worth voters.

247

FLORIDA BLOSSOMED in the arts during the 1950s, and Sarasota, with its Ringling Art Museum, was a leader. Hilton Leech, instructor at Amagansett Art School, holds a class *(above)* in landscape painting. Sarasota also became well known for music and drama.

SARASOTA attracted famous artists and writers after World War II. Finding the atmosphere agreeable, many stayed. Here are a few of them: MacKinlay Kantor *(left),* John D. MacDonald *(above); facing page, clockwise:* Syd Solomon, Ben Stahl, Irving Bendig, Richard Glendinning, and Thorton Utz. (Marth)

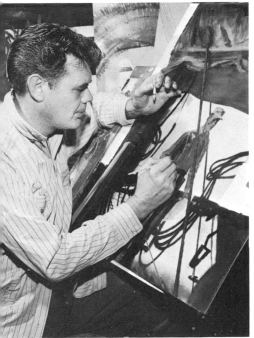

AFTER THE RETURN to full civilian production by industry following World War II, Florida began making an enormous growth, with construction at Miami Beach continuing the impetus begun in the 1930s but interrupted by the war. Construction of hotel row continued north of the Roney Plaza Hotel in the 1950s. The aerial *(above)* shows hotel row south from Forty-fourth Street in 1954.

MAJOR LUXURY hotel to be built at Miami Beach after the war, the Fontainbleau, rises between the ocean and Collins Avenue, in the block north of Forty-fourth Street. The mansion of the late Harvey Firestone, on whose estate the huge hotel rises, still stands when this photograph was made in 1954. The mansion was razed soon thereafter. (MBPD)

CHANGE FAILED to come to all communities alike after the war. Apalachicola was still a small town in the 1950s. Its greatest era was during the cotton boom before the Civil War. Naval stores and lumber were its principal exports during the half-century before the Depression. Although Apalachicola became famous for its oyster fisheries after World War II, it lacked potential for rapid growth. However, its discovery in the 1960s as a summer resort, because of its boating and fishing, would bring many people to the northwest Florida town. (SPA)

251

RURAL COUNTIES of north and northwest Florida tended to lose population after the war, as people left the countryside in pursuit of opportunities in the city. Lafayette County, smallest of Florida's sixty-seven counties, had 2,892 residents in 1970, compared with 3,440 in 1950. Some 800 live in Mayo, the county seat, whose courthouse *(below)* rises from among moss-draped liveoaks and cabbage palms. (SPA)

SPLENDID though it may be, in day or night setting, Florida's State Capitol resembles very little the original building completed in 1845. Even the east portico, or main entrance *(above)* which resembles that of the first building, is not original. The original portico was demolished for the addition of the east wing in 1922. The building was expanded in 1902, 1922, 1937, 1947, and again in 1972. The 1972 additions are part of a plan designed by Edward Durell Stone & Associates of New York and Reynolds, Smith & Hills of Jacksonville for a systematic development of a new Capitol Center. (SPA)

SNOW FELL on the State Capitol on February 13, 1958, exactly fifty-nine years after the snow storm of February 13, 1899. But it couldn't have been an ill omen, since neither date was on a Friday. The snow-laden tree is a magnolia. (SPA)

STATE BIRD of Florida is the mockingbird, but don't try to tell that to visitors who enjoy watching and photographing the comical pelican, as at St. Petersburg's municipal pier.

PIER 5, in Bayfront Park, was one of Miami's favorite places for tourists and local people alike, before it was razed in the 1960s for the Miamarina Yacht Basin and restaurant. Here a group of successful fishermen have their picture snapped beneath a day's catch. At Pier 5 you could buy filets of your favorite fish, cleaned and cut up as you watched, for pennies a pound. (Miami Herald)